# Contents

Copyright

Preface

Life of Karma     1

Chapter 2     9

Chapter 3     14

Chapter 4     18

Chapter 5     23

Chapter 6     27

Chapter 7     36

Chapter 8     41

Chapter 9     60

Chapter 10     63

Chapter 11     72

Chapter 12     79

Chapter 13     87

Chapter 14     103

Chapter 15     110

Chapter 16     128

Chapter 17     149

Chapter 18     153

Chapter 19                                    159

Acknowledgement                               175

# Preface

This book is based on actual true events and compiled from the author's life, from the beginnings of teenage life through the struggles with drugs, relationships, and victories of adulthood to funny little snippets and some outrageous stories and encounters.

He takes you through this journey from a young age, living in a small town in Denmark, being stuck with no way out, and to his start on a new chapter, moving to the UK with only the clothes on his back, making it through as a chef, and meeting some incredible and many time unsavory characters on the way, turning his life around only to get kicked down again and fighting back. Until he met his wife-to-be, emigrated to Australia, and then the battles to come. Starting all over again, with no friends or family around the darkest clouds, they are only coming closer to the real struggles they had just begun, alone in the land down under.

# Life of Karma

Our gym classes had the boys and girls in the same groups and having showers together. At one point, we had a beautiful Woman as a gym teacher. Sometimes, even she would have a shower in the same dressing rooms, so you would make sure to be in and out before she would arrive and get undressed.

This became very apparent to us one afternoon when one of our classmates got caught in the shower, and suddenly, the gym teacher walked past him and started showering.

Suddenly, he didn't want to leave the shower and had his back turned. When prompted to get dressed as class was about to start, he soon ran to his clothes with a solid erection. He tried desperately to hide it and get dressed before anyone noticed, but the laughter and pointing started once the first girl saw.

So we learned that if she was on duty, then get that shower done quickly, or else the ramification was horrific for your self-esteem.

I remember that incident vividly, even now, as an adult. It taught me always to be careful and aware of my surroundings. But my time at Rörvig Friskole wasn't all about the naked antics of teenagers. It was a unique experience where I learned valuable life lessons.

One of the things that stood out to me was the emphasis placed on learning through experience rather than just textbooks. We often went on nature walks and learned about the environment around us. We also had an annual camping trip where we would learn survival skills like starting a fire and building shelter.

But what I loved the most about Rörvig Friskole was the sense of community. It was a small school where everyone knew each other, and there was a strong emphasis on helping each other. I made some great friends there, who I still keep in touch with.

As I grew older, I started to appreciate the hippie vibe of the School. It was a refreshing change from the strict and state school style system I had come from after my parent's divorce, and the first School I arrived at was just not for me.

I got bullied a lot in the new School and never really fit in, so after one year, my mum arranged for me to attend the Alternative School, which only had about 120 pupils and most classes consisted of 10-15 students.

This new place suited me better, and most of this time, until I was 16, went pretty well; although I still got bullied, I had learned to fight back by now, so most of that got put in check with a swift kick to the gut.

Despite my troubled childhood, my time at the Alternative School was one of the best times in my life.

But growing up in the '90s had its perks, as well as learning life lessons; I got to enjoy a lot of the popular culture coming out that decade.

I remember I was a massive fan of the TV show Beverley Hills 90210 and even got my hair done like Dylan McKay from the show. I still have the photos as we speak. I also loved watching Inspector Gadget, Masters of the Universe, and Transformers - robots in disguise cartoons.

Although I got teased initially for having the Dylan hair, other people soon copied me.

It did get too much at one point as I would get teased because of my surname, and most kids then started calling me a variation of silly names, which got a rise out of me when it kept going for too long. So we decided that I would take my mum's surname to try and eliminate that part.

It helped, and it just wore off over time.

The School Rörvig Friskole is a (Lille Skole) Little School and operates differently from a regular state school.

It was more based on helping each other and working together; many classes would be structured with different categories, which felt more like a remnant from the 70s Hippie community.

There was always a lot of singing and group chats.

As I look back on those years, I can't help but chuckle at the naivety of it all. We were just kids going through puberty, trying to figure out our bodies and the world around us. But in that little Hippie School, where everyone was free to express themselves, it was hard not to get caught up in the moment.

I grew up in a small town in Denmark and remember living with my parents in a one-bedroom house they had purchased. I would help my dad do garden work and usually get into trouble.

I broke my legs twice at around five years old; the first time was after watching a Tarzan movie. I went straight out the back and laid a wooden beam across the basement stairway to climb across. I made it half away, and the wood and my heel bone broke.

The second time was playing in kindergarten, and after some heavy frost, the ground was like concrete when I jumped off a 3-meter tall wooden climbing frame and broke my leg again. I would climb anything I could get away with, so I would be expected to break something.

My parents divorced when I was around seven years old, and I would stay with my mother and see my dad every second weekend from then on.

## Denmark

The 1990s, Denmark was a fantastic free place; you could buy cigarettes and alcohol without a problem. The minimum age was 15, but that never got imposed.

Even at the local Video store, you could rent X-rated videos, and they were just out in the open, and no one had any problem with this. The counter where you pay would have numerous magazines displayed right in front of you, and some would be Playboy and other X-rated magazines, which was just considered normal. My grandmother would even get her weekly TV guide, and there would be a page 9 girl who would be full frontal nude, and she would sometimes say hey, check out her knockers or similar, or turn the page. It was a time when no one got offended about everyday life, natural naked people, etc.

Our School was super laidback as well. When you were 15, and your parents had signed a form, you were permitted to smoke in School at an allocated smoking table in the teacher's lounge. I recall the principal even bumming a cigarette here and there from students.

Even Beers at school parties were available for students over 15 years old.

As I entered 9th grade, I was excited about going to the UK with my classmates. It was the first time I would be away from my mother for over a week. The experience was going to be new and exciting. We spent our first day visiting the local youth center to meet the locals. I was initially nervous, but as soon as we got there, I realized they were just like us. They were friendly and welcoming.

The next day, I started my work experience with a local business. I worked with a mobile shop that would drive around the local area with produce and everyday shopping items like cheese, milk, and bread. My day started early, and I would help with the shop's inventory, loading and unloading the van, and helping customers with their shopping. I learned a lot about running a business from the family I was working with. They even invited me to their home to watch a Liverpool game on TV, and I was treated with the utmost respect. We had a great night being fed and pampered before returning to the church, where we stayed for the week.

We would take the bus to School, which was 7 kilometers away, and then take the bus back in the afternoon. One thing remained the same: my friend and I would head straight to the local Grill

Bar on our return. We would spend most of our afternoons playing arcade games in the local Grill bar, which was as high-tech as it got at that time. We could spend several hours playing and just watching other kids play to learn the game and how to beat it.

Stepping inside the grill bar was always a rush on the senses; a wave of smoky heat rushes to greet you. The scent of sizzling barbecue and freshly deep-fried chips wafts through the air, making your mouth water in anticipation. Your stomach grumbles hungrily, desperate for a taste of whatever delicious treats lie in wait. Still, as teenagers, we usually only had money to buy chips or hotdogs, as we needed our coins for the arcades.

We would move between three places in the early years, depending on what games were there: the two grill bars and a Chinese restaurant with an arcade area.

They were always competing and trying to get you to try the games before you chose.

One year, I beat all the high scores on the King of Fighters machine they had; I had hit the very last level and had to wait for the manager to show up, to confirm and give me my prize. A bag of chips and a drink was a big thing because I had beaten the game. To have your name on the screen was a huge thing, as they stayed on until beaten by another player or even after the manager had turned the arcades off at night.

So many times, other teenagers would only know you by your three initials, which you could put in when you beat a high score. I used my middle name and the name I was known as by my friends. "R.Y.E"

## Field Fire Troubles

At some point, I was roaming with this older kid who would always get us into trouble. That day, we had started a small fireplace in a shed on a field behind my grandparents' house. The next day, I heard that there had been a massive fire the fire brigade had attended, and the shed had burned down. For years, I felt guilty about it and never told anyone. It wasn't until 1999 that this came up in a chat with my friends. A friend of mine said that he had gone back later that evening with the other guy, and they restarted the fire, and then it got out of control, and they ran away. So, for over 12 years, I felt super guilty about it, and then it wasn't even my fault! Who needs enemies when you have friends like that?

"You knew this whole time?" I asked him, struggling to keep my voice steady.

As the memories flooded back, I couldn't help but feel angry at my supposed friend's betrayal. How could he let me take the blame for something he had done?

He nodded, looking down at his hands. "I'm sorry, man. I should have told you sooner. But I didn't want to get in trouble."

But the anger soon dissipated and was replaced with a sense of relief. I could finally let go of the guilt weighing me down all those years.

We all laughed and breathed a sigh of relief that the past had passed and we were now together.

## Town celebrations

I got pulled into a brawl during our town's annual street party. A group of older kids, who had been drinking heavily, didn't like my playful banter and decided to give me a beating. Two of them rushed at me and began punching me in the head. Thankfully, my friend intervened and hit one of them as he ran past, giving me enough time to escape without any significant injuries besides a bruised ego. We hid in the crowd for the remainder of the evening, which was easy, given how many people were at the street party.

The Street party was like a carnival with rides and games, and it was proper carnie people who were travelers moving from town to town and looked after each other. So, there would always be fights late at night when the drinks had been flowing heavily. They were defending themselves against scrutiny of people losing money on games, etc., but this was always a highlight for the year, a whole week of bumper cars, pokie machines, and all the typical games to win teddy bears, cheap toys and candy everywhere the eye looked.

Despite the brawl earlier, my friend and I decided to make the most of the evening. We walked around, trying our luck at various games and enjoying the festive atmosphere. The smell of cotton candy and popcorn filled the air, and the distant sounds of laughter and excited screams from the rides could echo through the streets.

We were drawn to the bumper car ride as the night went on. It was always a favorite of ours, and tonight was no exception. We waited in line, watching as the cars bumped into each other and sparks flew. Finally, it was our turn.

We climbed into our cars, grinning at each other in anticipation. We were off as soon as the ride started, racing around and crashing into each other. It was pure adrenaline, and we couldn't stop laughing. For a few minutes, we forgot about the earlier brawl and the trouble that could be lurking in the crowd.

They had spotted us, but it was probably just a reaction to attack for them. By now, they had forgotten about it. They were looking for more beers and different trouble to entertain their drunken minds. As we came out from the bumper cars, we saw them having started another fight with a group of adults their size, so we were of no concern to them anymore.

Another tradition would be the celebration of Fastelavn, which comes from the Roman Catholic tradition of Lent, which was a 40-day fast, and the festivities would had before that started.

But when I was a child, it would consist of a day with a carnival in School, and everyone would dress up. We would line up and take turns hitting a barrel with treats usually decorated with cats.

The person who beats open the barrel and makes the sweets fall out is proclaimed *kattekonge* ("king of cats") and coronated with a shiny paper crown. The game continues until somebody knocks down the last board of the barrel. This person will then receive a smaller crown and the title of *kattedronning* ("queen of cats").

The sweets were then shared amongst the children. That is because, back in the day, there used to be real cats in those barrels. The custom aimed to drive the evil spirits away (people used to believe cats were connected to evil).

So the school day would be fun and games, and the second part was the Rattling.

All the kids walked door to door, rattling their money tins and singing songs, expecting to get money or candy.

Generally, coins would be collected, and then you would move on to the next house. This could be profitable for a young person, especially if you put the work in and kept going for hours.

# Chapter 2

## False Accusations

### 1989

I heard a knock on the door that night, and my mother called me to the kitchen. Two police officers stood there with stern faces, asking me if I had broken into someone's house and caused some damage. I denied doing anything of that sort since it was not something I would do and not by myself—I was usually more of a follower than a leader in matters like these. Plus, I had been with my dad 16 Kilometers away the entire weekend- it would've been impossible for me to have gotten there and back on a bicycle. The officers eventually left, but my mum still scolded me.

The next day, my cousin offered to take me to speak to the family who'd accused me of breaking in. When we arrived, the kid who claimed to have seen me enter didn't even recognize me! After talking with their parents, we found out that this same boy had committed the crime; his own house was right next door to where he'd broken in! Problem solved.

As I walked away from the house of the family who had falsely accused me of breaking in, I felt a sense of relief wash over me. It was like a huge weight had been lifted off my shoulders. I couldn't believe someone could be so cruel as to accuse me of something I had not done. It was a good thing that the truth had finally come out.

But as I made my way down the street, I couldn't shake off the feeling that something was not quite right. Then, I saw the boy who had falsely accused me, walking right towards me. He had a sheepish look like he had been caught red-handed. I knew that this was my chance to confront him.

"Hey, you!" I shouted as I walked over to him. "What were you thinking, falsely accusing me like that?"

The boy looked down at his feet, unable to meet my gaze. "I'm sorry, He apologized profusely, saying that he had lied because he was too scared to admit that he had done it. He begged for my forgiveness and would make sure that everyone would know it wasn't me and that it was his doing.

We parted ways, and it felt like a win, and I never heard anything about this matter again. So he did keep his word after all, to which I applaud him.

∞ ∞ ∞

## Accidental Ego Collision

I was probably thirteen years old when I got my first brand new push bike with drop handlebars, and I was cruising down through our town, picking up some good speed.

As I passed a soccer field with at least twenty people scattered in different groups playing ball, a familiar face called out from the crowd—it was my friend who lived across the road. I waved back, smiling. But the next thing I knew, I had collided with a large green metal container that blended perfectly with its surroundings of overgrown bushes and climbing plants on the walls next to where it was standing.

The impact was loud and violent. With an almighty crash, I found myself hanging off the top of it. My front fork was damaged beyond repair. What hurt, however, were the laughs from other players who had seen me sway towards the container from fifty meters away.

Thankfully, I survived unscathed, except my ego was bruised. Now I needed to buy a new front fork for two hundred Danish kroner (a lot for us, considering we only had a little money).

Unfortunately, a few days later, I slammed into a metal bar near the train tracks because I did not tighten the brakes properly after repairs. Telling my mum I needed another two hundred Danish kroner didn't go well.

But the fall was worth it, or so I thought. You see, as I lay there on the ground, holding my mangled bike, a girl from my School ran over to me. Her name was Anja, and I had always thought she was out of my league. But as she helped me to my feet, I noticed how she looked at me - with concern and maybe even a hint of admiration.

"Are you okay?" she asked, her hand still on my arm.

I nodded, feeling a surge of confidence. "Yeah, I'm fine. Just a little shaken up."

Anja smiled, and I swear my Heart skipped a beat. "You're pretty brave," she said. "I don't know many guys who would take a spill like that and still get back up."

I grinned, feeling like a hero. "Well, you know me. I'm tough."

Anja laughed and shook her head. "Yeah, I can see that."

From that moment on, we would meet whenever she was around the football field. We even snuck a kiss once, but we never got any further as she lived in another town. After these few encounters/dates, we never saw each other again.

As I walked back home, pushing my broken bike alongside me, I couldn't help but feel like a complete idiot. How could I have been so careless not once but twice in a matter of days? My pride took a severe hit, and I could already hear the teasing from my friends at School.

But then my spirits would return after thinking of Anja and how she made me feel, which would trump the bike crash anytime.

## The Moped Mishap

This evening, I played with two older boys, and we were all full of fun ideas. We left my mum's apartment on the estate and swiped a 10-meter garden hose, thinking it might be useful later. As we made our way down the road, we spotted a shopping trolley wedged in a hedge. It seemed perfect for riding further down the road, so we grabbed it.

We kept competing with each other to be the most impressive as we approached an area where wooden planters blocked off the street. Cars had to turn around, but only bikes could continue past the School. Someone suggested jamming the shopping trolley into the gap between the planters to block off the rest of the street and then using the garden hose to keep it secure.

As we finished tying the garden hose, we heard a moped whizzing behind us and warned each other. We dove over a fence into an enormous grassy field surrounded by bushes. We just managed to disappear before the moped flew past.

It didn't see our barricade at all, so it kept going straight through the planter opening - only this time, a metal cart was stuck in there, held together by a garden hose! The rider crashed into the cart, and the moped ground to a halt.

The rider yelled profanities and multiple threats, then restarted his moped with a bit of effort. It sounded like it was running choppily now, but he used the headlights to search the bushes where we were hiding.

One of the older boys was still very close to the accident site as he had been the last to make it over the fence. The other one and I were around twenty meters away from him and in complete cover.

We all panicked, wondering if we should run or stay put when the driver shone his headlights through the greenery. He then screamed maniacally and tossed a shopping trolley over the fence towards us. Miraculously, it became lodged in the branches of the bush right above our friend, who was just a few meters away from where the angry guy was, who thankfully remained motionless beneath it.

After a few more warnings, the man drove off on his rickety moped, and only after he had gone did we muster up enough courage to start laughing about what had happened before heading home fast.

Walking briskly back to my mum's apartment, we recounted the night's events and how we nearly got caught. Suddenly, my Heart skipped a beat as I realized that my mum's boyfriend, Nikolaj, was sitting on the porch waiting for us.

Nikolaj had always been a wild card, and I wondered if he liked me. He stood up and walked towards us, his eyes fixed on the shopping trolley we were dragging along.

"What are you boys up to?" he asked, his voice laced with suspicion.

I could feel my cheeks turning red as I tried to devise an excuse, but one of the older boys spoke up before I could say anything.

"We found this shopping trolley on the street," he said, lying smoothly. "We were just playing around with it."

Nikolaj arched an eyebrow but didn't say anything. He walked past us and picked up the garden hose we had left lying on the ground.

We quickly said goodbye, and the other two disappeared into the dark to return home. And I moved inside rapidly, saying goodnight to my mum, then straight to bed and locked the door. I never got a response from Nikolaj, so either he bought my story, or maybe he had my back after all.

# Chapter 3

## Staying On Target

### 1990

My friend had invited me to try sports shooting as he was really into it, and learning to shoot rifles sounded fun.

I remember the first day, the instructors were keen to see if I was returning as I had scored 186 out of 200 on the first attempt, and they wanted me to stick with it.

They soon after gave me a private instructor and free ammunition as part of their program. The national championship was coming up soon, and the club wanted me to join their team of four talented shooters.

I was thrilled at the offer and eagerly accepted. The team consisted of three seasoned veterans and myself, the newcomer. They welcomed me with open arms and shared their knowledge and experience.

We trained tirelessly in preparation for the championship, spending hours at the shooting range daily. My skills improved vastly under their guidance, and I quickly adapted to shooting under pressure. I was determined to make my team proud and bring home the championship trophy.

My coach was an expert marksman who advised me to use Russian ammo for its precision rather than Lapua's more popular brand; I quickly began consistently scoring 196 out of 200. I had been chosen to represent the club at the nationals.

As the championship day approached, my nerves began to take hold. I had never shot in front of such a big crowd before, and the thought of letting down my team weighed heavily on my mind. But I was determined to stay on target and bring home the trophy.

On the day of the championship, the atmosphere was electric. The air was thick with the smell of gunpowder, and the sound of rifle shots echoed through the range. I took deep breaths and tried to calm my nerves as I stepped up to take my first shot.

I aimed down the barrel of my rifle and focused on my target. My heart was pounding in my chest as I slowly squeezed the trigger. The shot rang out through the range, and I watched the bullet hit the target dead center.

I was off to a great start, but the nerves took hold, and I ended up with a score average of 196, which was my PB, so I stuck to my skills and did what I could for the team.

It was a considerable experience, and having to travel to the other side of the country and perform in an unfamiliar environment, then seeing the shooting range with hundreds of teams and over fifty shooters all firing at once was amazing! We placed ninth overall out of more than 200 teams, and everyone returned home feeling proud of their accomplishment.

## Confirmation

Traditionally, in Denmark, you will be Konfirmated at 14 to 15 years old; among those Christians practicing teenaged confirmation, the practice may be perceived as a "coming of age" rite—the Danish protestant equivalent to Bat Mitzvah or first communion.

We never really went to church, and part of the ritual involved going to the local Priests house for 2 hours each Thursday before school started, so from 6 am to 8 am, which meant getting up before sunrise to go there and then listen to the priest for 2 hours, this was heavy duty work mentally, especially when I didn't understand my faith back then.

Most kids would do it because everyone else was, the parents made them, and the main bonus was the party and the gifts supplied on the day, usually in the thousands of dollars and presents.

Confirmation preparation most often occurs in the rectory or a room close to the church. The teaching consists of at least 48 lessons, but according to the Ministry of the Church, it must consist of up to 56 lessons. For the preparation, the priest teaches the Bible, the church's rituals, hymns, history, and role in modern society. The purpose is to strengthen the confirmands' knowledge of the Christian faith. Still, it must also inspire and guide them in their choice to confirm their baptism. A priest may well demand that the confirmands must participate in a certain number of services to be verified. If you do not meet the preparation requirements, the priest can reject students from being confirmed.

So we had a nonfirmation.

What is the difference between confirmation and nonfirmation? Whereas confirmation is a church act associated with religion, a non-confirmation is a kind of civil confirmation that someone chooses if they do not want to be confirmed in the church but prefer a non-religious alternative to the confirmation.

The general similarity between a confirmation and a non-confirmation is that the celebration symbolizes the transition from child to adult and, most often, in the form of a party with speeches, songs, and gifts - religious or not.

The whole family comes around and has a big celebration. You would all spend the day together eating and talking. The kids would retreat to separate areas to look at the presents and maybe have their first alcoholic drink.

The primary present I got was from my mother; it was a Commodore Amiga 500 Computer, which was the best you could get for playing Games at the time. It had 500 kb RAM, which was part of the name, and this could be upgraded to a fantastic 1024 of RAM (1 MB) to play more resource-heavy games. The 512ram upgrade is the size of 2x an A3 book by today's standards and with the intelligence of nothing available, as we now operate in GB = 1000 Mb and the Amiga had Half an Mb.

But at the time, this was as cool as it could get, and we would spend hours hanging out, playing games with friends and sharing games between us.

# Chapter 4

## Air guitar Championships

### 1991

At our youth club "Freden" in 1991, we held a local Air Guitar competition to qualify for the National Championship. Most of us would head to the local servo on these Friday nights and buy alcohol since there was no age limit on purchasing cigarettes and alcohol. We often got 'Gammel Dansk,' a Danish bitters created in 1961 and flavored with secret herbs and spices like star anise, nutmeg, ginger, laurel, gentian, Seville orange, cinnamon, and more. The 38% alcohol hit hard, especially when temperatures were low.

As the competitors gathered on stage, the smell of Gammel Dansk lingered in the air. The crowd cheered as the first contestant, a skinny kid named Tim, stepped up to the mic stand and began shredding an imaginary guitar. He swayed to the beat of the imaginary drums, and his fingers flew over the frets of his invisible guitar. The crowd went wild, cheering and clapping as he finished his performance.

Next up was Lily, who looked like she had just stepped off the set of a rock music video. She twirled her long hair in the air as she mimicked playing an electric guitar. Her movements were so fluid it was as if she was playing a real guitar. The crowd loved it and cheered her on as she finished her set.

It was then that I had a plan. I wanted to make my performance stand out, so at the competition, I arranged for my friends to create a path to the mirror wall when I gave them a nod during my guitar solo. Then, I ran up towards the wall, took one step up, and jumped onto the dance floor while spinning around, landing on my knees and sliding towards the judges, which excited the crowd and judges. Finally, due to what must have been the influence of 'Gammel Dansk,' I tore open my button shirt right in front of the female judge! Buttons flew everywhere as this indeed secured me the win!

As the crowd erupted into applause and cheers, I couldn't help but feel like a rockstar. The female judge blushed and looked away, but I knew I had impressed her with my bold move. I was elated as the emcee announced my name as the winner of the Air Guitar Championships.

As I walked off the stage, my friends greeted me with high-fives and pats on the back. I couldn't wait to attend the National Championships and show my skills to a larger audience.

The next few weeks of practicing and preparing for the big competition were a blur. I spent hours perfecting my air guitar moves and developing new tricks to wow the judges and the crowd.

Later that night, we laughed about it while reliving each moment.

Upon qualifying for the National championships, a bus was arranged for local supporters to attend the event in Copenhagen. I went with my uncle, who knew the main act of the evening – Dr. Baker, a Dance DJ who was all the rage at that time. When we got to the venue, there were over 1000 people inside.

The competition was intense, with 20 participants, most of whom were like me: everyday people who had made it to the next level. Then, a few had planned this for a very long time and knew what they were doing. The stage was well-lit so that I couldn't hide; all the prizes on shelves near the only visible wall ruined my signature move of jumping off the wall.

However, I hadn't lost my heart and still had a surprise attack planned with my friends storming the stage and tearing apart my shirt. While it affected the audience, take note that if you plan to do this too, use lightweight fabric, which is easier to rip than cotton! Ultimately, I came sixth out of twenty competitors, winning prizes such as a Swatch double phone -the hottest item back then.

Despite not winning the National Air Guitar Championship, I was still on cloud nine. The competition had been fierce, and I had given it my all. As I left the venue, my uncle clapped me on the back and said, "You may not have won, but you sure left an impression on the judges and the audience. You're a winner in my book."

His words meant a lot to me, and I felt proud of my accomplishments. I had come a long way from the shy kid who used to hang out at the youth club, and now I had a taste of what it felt like to be a rock star.

Over the next few weeks, my friends and I relived the competition, laughing and joking about our performances. We may not have been the best air guitarists in the country, but we had the time of our lives.

∞∞∞

### Stockholm Football Cup.

As a teenager, I always played a lot of football. We were invited to a massive tournament in Stockholm, Sweden, this year.

We had a solid team this year and looked forward to going away for a long weekend.

The opening game was against PARMA, the previous three years winners from Italy.

We were playing the same day as the opening game for the tournament. We were warming up behind the main stadium for the opening game, which held 3,500 spectators. There was a massive commotion for everyone getting ready and spectators arriving for the opening game.

Our coach had told us about 15 minutes before our game; we would get picked up by a bus and be driving to the field where our game was taking place.

As we were warming up, I couldn't help but feel a sense of excitement and nerves building up inside me. This was the biggest tournament we had ever participated in, and we were up against the reigning champions in our opening game. Looking around at my teammates, I could see they were under pressure. So we warmed up and got ready.

The bus arrived, and it was not like any bus we had seen before. It was huge and shiny and looked expensive.

It was not until we walked onto the bus that we saw the opposition players who looked huge compared to us, all wearing the same socks, footy boots, and outfits, tanned and immaculate hair, giving us the evil stare as we entered the bus; this was when we knew something was up, and our trainer confirmed that we were indeed playing the opening game against the three years in a row Italian Champions Parma.

The shock set in, what were we up against, and then we got told that the luxury bus would drive us from behind the stadium and directly onto the field where the 3500 spectators were waiting and, when we stopped, then run out in a perfect line and stand in front of the crowd and wait until our names were called out over the speakers and then stand forward and give a wave to the crowd.

We were blown away and petrified simultaneously, but we were flying on cloud nine when the crowd erupted when we were called onto the pitch, and the adrenalin kicked in.

We ended up beating them 3-0, and our tournament journey was off to the most fantastic start we ever imagined.

After that stunning victory against Parma, our team was buzzing with energy and confidence. We strutted around Stockholm like we owned the place, heads held high, and chests puffed out. We had a swagger to our step that everyone noticed, even the locals. It was like we had become mini-celebrities in our own right.

But, as the tournament progressed, we started to feel the pressure build up again. We were up against some tough opponents, all eager to take us down a peg or two. Our coach saw the shift in our attitude and knew he needed to do something to keep the team focused.

He gathered us together after a practice session and spoke to us in a low, measured voice. "Lads, I know you're feeling good after that first game, but don't let it get to your heads. We've got a long way to go in this tournament, and we need to stay focused on each game as it comes. We need to play like we started, against the champions, with respect for their skill but with confidence that we can beat the team we are playing.

We made it to the Quarterfinals and had a fantastic time. Still, that opening game will always stand out as one unique experience, and the crowd cheering us on was out of this world.

As the Stockholm Football Cup ended, our team returned home to a hero's welcome. We had exceeded everyone's expectations and had brought pride to our small town. But as the excitement died, we knew we couldn't rest on our laurels. We had to keep pushing ourselves to be better, to achieve more.

And that's when the Danish national indoor Football tournament came up. We had been training hard and were eager to show off our skills on a national level. The contest was fierce, with some of the best teams from all over Denmark competing against each other.

Our first game was challenging against a team that had won the tournament the previous year. But we weren't intimidated, knowing that we had already beaten the reigning champions of the Stockholm Football Cup. We played with the same intensity and focus and won the game by a narrow margin.

From there, we went on a winning streak, taking down some of the best teams in the tournament and ending up being crowned the sixth-best team in the nation.

# Chapter 5

## Quick Escape

### 1992

In Denmark, you can drive a Moped from the age of 16. You need to get a license, and they didn't have a number plate when I grew up, so the advantage was that the police had to catch/stop you for you to get a ticket.

Most Mopeds are 50cc and are legally allowed to go 35 km, but some would do 50 km after being driven in for a while.

But then you have several options to tune them to drive faster. When I purchased a Puch Monza 3 gears, which already had some modifications and extra upgrades, it was doing 110km.

I never thought I'd have to use the speed of my Puch Monza for anything more than just racing down the empty country roads. But when I saw the flashing lights behind me, I knew I had to put my skills to the test.

I revved the engine and took off down the street, weaving in and out of traffic. My heart raced as I looked in my rearview mirror and saw the police car getting closer and closer. I knew I had to lose them, or I would end up with a hefty ticket or, worse, get caught for my illegal modifications.

I hit the gas and swerved onto a side street, the police car hot on my tail. I could hear the sirens blaring, and I knew it was only a matter of time before they caught up to me. But I wasn't ready to give up yet.

I spotted a narrow alleyway ahead and quickly turned, feeling the bike skid beneath me. I narrowly avoided and outran the police several times, and knowing the local area made it easy as you could drive down small laneways and places cars wouldn't go.

The most memorable time was when I drove up one of the main roads in town. As I was passing the local City hall, I knew they were chasing me, so I pulled into a side street, quickly turned in behind a fence behind my friend's house, and sat still until the police car raced past. Then my friend's mother came running out, shouting who are the police chasing?

I told her it was me, and she replied," Quick, roll the bike into the shed," so I did, and she locked the garage door and told me to rush inside and lay low inside until they stopped searching.

I did as she said, feeling my heart racing as I heard the police car sirens getting closer and closer. I could hear them searching the area, but I remained, hidden away in my friend's house. It was a nerve-wracking experience, but I knew I had to wait it out to avoid getting caught.

Hours passed, and I stayed low, waiting for any sign that it was safe to come out. So, for the next few hours, we saw them drive up and down the street looking for me, and I had a nice dinner with my friend's family, waited for darkness, and then drove the bike home quickly.

Finally, we heard the sound of the police car driving away, the sirens fading into the distance. I sighed in relief, knowing that I had escaped once again.

As I left the house, my friend's mother greeted me with a smile. "You made it," she said, patting me on the back. "I knew you could do it."

I thanked her for her help, grateful for her quick thinking and bravery. Without her, I would have been caught for sure.

## Denmark winning Euro 92

Denmark's qualification for Euro 92 makes the subsequent

triumph in the competition such a peculiarity since they did not earn their place at the tournament in the traditional manner.

They had finished second in their qualification group behind Yugoslavia after winning six games, drawing one and losing one.

Yugoslavia was due to compete in the final stage of the European Championship. Still, the country was suspended from competitive football by FIFA and UEFA following the outbreak of the Yugoslav Wars.

As such, Denmark, as the next-best qualifier from the group, took their place at the tournament. All the players were being called home from holidays, and most were not training for weeks.

The entire country was excited that we made it, and then, after getting through the group stage, the whole thing just got out of control. There were stories of how the players were giving it everything they had to win this, and one player was known to have left his beard grow and wouldn't shave until they lost a game.

The excitement of Denmark's unexpected success at Euro 92 was palpable. The country was buzzing with anticipation and support for their national team. The players had been called back from their holidays. They were training hard, determined to make the most of this unexpected opportunity.

The bearded player, whose facial hair had grown long and wild, symbolized the team's determination. He had become a hero to the fans, who cheered him on with every pass, every tackle, and every shot on goal.

The team's success had also brought them under intense scrutiny. The media was eager to follow their every move, and the players were constantly in the spotlight. But they remained focused and determined, knowing they had the chance to make history.

As the tournament progressed, the Danes continued to impress. They got through their group on a slim margin, beating the Frence in the last group game to secure the runners-up spot and advance to the knockout stage, where they faced tough opponents in the semi-finals. But they refused to be intimidated, playing with passion and skill.

It was the semi-finals, and we beat the Dutch team, which was outrageous as they had so many world-class players. Still, after a 2-2 draw, it went into a penalty shot out and with our talisman Peter Schmeichel, one of the best goalkeepers ever known, beat them after Schmeichel saved a penalty from one of the most feared strikers at the time, Marco Van Basten.

The final was against Germany, the current world champions.

The story was that they had booked their flights home to Germany so close to the end of the game that if it went into overtime, they would miss their flights, so they were super confident they would beat us easily and then go home to celebrate.

Unfortunately for them, we had the Danish Viking spirit flowing. We beat the Germans 2-0 in the final, and then our country was having the biggest party I have ever witnessed.

Every person in every town was out on the street cheering, drinking beers, and celebrating with their neighbors long into the night.

In the capital, we saw more than half a million people assembled in the main square to celebrate the victors of Europe on the night on every TV channel.

The victory was a momentous occasion for Denmark, bringing the country together in a way they had never experienced before. The streets were lined with flags and banners, and the air was thick with the scent of beer and joy.

The players were greeted as heroes as they returned home from the tournament. They were given a ticker-tape parade through the streets of Copenhagen, with thousands of fans lining the route to cheer them on.

# Chapter 6

## Community Youth Party

*1993*

Several times per year, there would be a huge indoor stadium party in a town called Gislinge.

This was a massive event, and we all planned to arrive in groups by train and car. The train ride could be compared to the old American movie Warriors; we were at the first station on the train line, and at every stop, another group of teenagers would jump onboard, and all the town dynamics would be exaggerated because of old confrontations between couples, football games or any other petty hate which could be used to start a fight, especially because alcohol and drugs were involved. So, getting to the final destination without trouble was not likely, and therefore, everyone always stuck together and moved in groups. The train ride was chaotic. Every time the train stopped, more teenagers would pile on, adding to the already crowded space. At one point, a group of guys from a rival town started throwing insults at us. One of my friends, a tall and muscular guy named Kim, took offense to their taunts and squared up to them. I could feel the tension in the air, and I was sure a fight was about to break out. But before anything could happen, the train lurched forward, and the moment was lost.

As we stepped off the train, a wave of excitement washed over me. The music from the party echoed through the station, and I could feel the bass thumping in my chest. My friends and I had been planning this night for weeks, and now we were finally here.

We made our way through the crowded streets, past groups of rowdy teenagers drinking and smoking. The air was thick with the smell of weed and sweat, and I couldn't help but feel a little nervous as it was always a crazy night.

As we reached the stadium entrance and pushed our way inside, all my worries disappeared. The atmosphere was electric - lights flashing, bodies writhing, music pumping It was like stepping into a different world, one where all the rules were different and anything could happen.

Once inside the stadium, the party would take its course. Most people would just enjoy the loud music and company, and then later, the trouble would start again; over one thousand teens, drunk was a recipe for disaster, and when emotions between girls and boys crossed paths, fights would break out, usually quickly stopped by the massive security presence.

Still, people would be left for the pickings outside if they didn't know the deal.

As the night wore on, I found myself getting more and more intoxicated. I couldn't remember how many drinks I had, but it didn't matter. All that mattered was the music, the people, and the adrenaline rushing through my veins.

The previous year, my friend had been in a heated altercation concerning a girl, which had ended with the other party shooting him in the face with a starter pistol. The ensuing burns were not severe enough to require medical attention. However, they did leave an impression on all of us. With this in mind, I tracked down some sketchy acquaintances from over the years, and we went out looking for the guy.

The chaos outside was even more intense than inside the stadium. The air was thick with smoke from cigarettes and joints. People were screaming, laughing, and shouting at each other, their voices blending into a frenzied cacophony. I felt the adrenaline rush through my body as I followed my sketchy acquaintances through the crowd, scanning the faces of everyone we passed.

And then, out of nowhere, a hand reached out and grabbed my

shoulder. I spun around, ready to fight, but it was Christian, an old friend who had heard what was going down and was there to help look for the perpetrator which we had just found before the security guards had turned up.

The interrogation was brief, and he was immediately asked about his attack on our friend. He was backed into a corner, and I could see he had a knife hidden in his hand, ready for anyone to make a move. I edged around him slowly while he was distracted talking to someone else. Then I kicked the hand holding the knife before we subdued him. Security had witnessed everything and intervened before we could take control of the situation. They found the knife but decided against stirring more conflict between us, advising us to part ways amicably.

Unfortunately, taking two different paths around the stadium led everyone to the same destination on the other side. Our friend didn't have time to realize what was happening until it was too late, and he got a harsh reminder of how people are treated when they pull a weapon in a one-on-one fight.

Soon enough, we returned to the party and enjoyed the beers, girls, and music.

This was just one of many fights, and at some point, gangs had started to turn up in large groups, all dressed in their attire; one group was known as the Little Greys and would all be wearing black, grey, white chequered flannel shirts. So then every town would stick together more, and fights became more group fights than individual punch-ups.

It was pretty common to meet a girl on these nights and hook up for the night and then not meet again, and this is where some fights would break out, as there were no mobile phones or social media, so scorned people would see this person at the next event and then get upset when A. they didn't recognize them or B. they saw them with someone else.

The night was getting late, and the party was reaching its peak. I was dancing with a girl, my arms around her waist, and her hands were exploring my body. We were both lost in the rhythm of the music, and I could feel the heat rising between us.

As the song ended, she leaned in and whispered in my ear, "Do you want to go somewhere more private?"

I took her hand without hesitation, and we went outside the stadium. The cool night air hit me, and I could feel the alcohol starting to take its toll. We found a corner where we could still hear the music, and she wrapped her arms around my neck. Our lips met, and I could taste the alcohol on her tongue.

As our clothes started coming off, I was lost in the moment.

∞∞∞

## End Of Season Shenanigans

Playing on the local football team was always a great bonding experience, especially when we had home games and our friends and families came to support us. Afterward, it was tradition to have some beers and play dice or other games as a way of celebrating.

I recall the end-of-season game particularly well when we were promoted to the next tier. The beer flowed into the changing rooms until the crates reached the ceiling! Then we went straight to the video store, where we purchased more alcohol before heading to O'Malley's Pub.

At the video store, one of my teammates suggested I should try to steal a life-size cardboard cutout of Arnold Schwarzenegger from the True Lies movie. Despite me feeling hesitant at first, he encouraged me to go along with it--all I needed was enough courage to walk out without looking suspicious. So that's exactly what I did! I picked up Arnie, tucked him under my arm, waved goodbye to everyone in the store, and walked right out.

As the night went on and our group of rowdy football players continued to celebrate, it seemed as though Arnold was enjoying the festivities just as much as we were. Before long, someone suggested we take him out for a night on the town, and we all agreed that it was a fantastic idea.

We piled into our cars, Arnold included, and headed to the nearest strip club. As we walked in, Arnold drew stares from the dancers and patrons alike. But we didn't care. We were having the time of our lives, and Arnold was our mascot for the night.

It was in the early hours of the morning that we realized we had lost Arnold. We retraced our steps, but he was nowhere to be found. We were all slightly disappointed, but we figured someone else must have found him and taken him on their own wild adventure.

Then suddenly, out of nowhere on the empty streets, Kristian, our goalkeeper, comes around the corner with Arnie's arm in arm, and we all erupt in joyful cheers. We surrounded Kristian, patting him on the back and thanking him for bringing Arnold back to us.

We eventually found ourselves at the captain's abode, where the festivities continued until the dawn of a new day. Everywhere I looked, Arnie was in the thick of it, beaming with pride as he held court.

## Metallica 1993

It was my first significant concert: Metallica. My two best buddies and I drove to the venue with my friend at the wheel—he had attended some concerts before, and so led the way.

We arrived at a football stadium in Copenhagen, with 25,000 people eagerly awaiting the acts.

My friend was ready to party; decked out in a torn shirt and a headband, he radiated alpha-male energy. We pushed through the crowd to get past the gates into the stadium, where various tents had been set up, offering merchandising, snacks, beer, etc. Then there was the stage: larger than life, with more speakers than I'd ever seen. Thousands of people were streaming into it from all directions, buzzing with anticipation for what was about to come.

As we got to our seats, the adrenaline started to kick in. My heart was pounding, my palms were sweaty, and I could feel the butterflies in my stomach. I was nervous yet excited, and I knew this would be a night to remember.

As the lights dimmed, the crowd erupted into cheers. The opening act began to play, and we all swayed to the music, singing along to the lyrics.

The Cult and Suicidal Tendencies opened for Metallica, setting off wild cheers among the fans. But it was when Metallica took to the stage the real magic happened with "Creeping Death."

The music was so loud it vibrated through my entire body, and I could feel the bass drum beating in my chest. The energy was electric, and the crowd was absolutely insane. People were moshing, jumping, and screaming along, and for at least ten minutes, I didn't touch the ground as people surged forward to get closer to their idols.

Eventually, we managed to make our way backward in the crowd and got a better view of the show.

My friend found himself thrown into the midst of a raging storm of skinheads and pushed around wildly until one of them was knocked to the ground. My friend stepped on the head of an enormous skinhead. Time seemed to stand still as my friend stood there in terror, expecting death to come at any moment when suddenly he saw the savage stand up and open its eyes and gaze at him. A crazed expression was etched onto its face. Still, he nodded and uttered the words "It's all good" before head banging with newfound ferocity. My friend realized his luck and quickly scrambled away before he changed his mind.

As Metallica continued to shred through their set, I couldn't help but feel alive. The energy was contagious, and I found myself head banging and screaming along with the lyrics. It was like nothing I had ever experienced before.

The lights flashed, illuminating the lead singer's face as he let out a fierce howl. The crowd went wild, and I found myself pushed forward once again. But this time, I didn't mind. I was caught up in the moment, and nothing could bring me down.

As the night went on, the music became more intense. The bass pounded through my body, and I could feel every note reverberating in my soul. Metallica was in their element, and the crowd was right there with them, raising their fists and screaming at the top of their lungs.

It was pure, unadulterated chaos, and I loved every second of it.

My friend had hit the hungry stage and marched through the crowd, his eyes a window to his ravenous hunger. He was dressed in garb typical of a guy from the chainsaw massacre, a long swirling headband setting off his fiery gaze. The collective energy of the masses seemed to part as he approached, allowing him to pass like a wave cresting in a roiling sea. His movements were made with steady confidence, and those who complained or attempted to impede his progress quickly backed off at the sight of his burning glare. We followed closely behind, taking up our own space in the tent and ordering our meals with haste. Before we knew it, we had all finished our food and exited quickly, leaving many disgruntled people behind, their scowls falling silent at the sight of my companion's unbridled determination.

We made our way to a raised area on top of the seating, where a walkway lined with gravel overlooked the stadium and gave us a great view of the concert and the crowd. We found a spot to sit, eat, and take in the atmosphere without worrying about being trampled in the mosh pit.

Suddenly, we noticed an individual who clearly had been dabbling in some heavier substances staggering towards us. As if drawn by some strange force, he began to hang off one of the light poles dangerously suspended over the crowd below. We watched in horror as his swinging caused the pole to lose its cover and crash into the people sitting underneath, inciting a fierce brawl between all involved. But this drugged-up hippie didn't care too much for a few black eyes before he left them for another unsuspecting victim.

The chaos only added to the excitement of the night, and

Metallica continued to play on, utterly unfazed by the madness that was unfolding below. The intense energy of the crowd only seemed to fuel them, and the music grew louder and more intense with each passing moment.

As the night wore on, my friends and I found ourselves lost in time, completely caught up in the music and the energy around us. We head banged and screamed, still completely lost in the moment. But as we prepare to leave, a trio of intoxicated girls can be heard discussing how long the queue for the portaloo's is. One suggests they squat in the hedge behind us. Every other man at this gig has now taken up the offer that was feasible three hours prior, and the urine-soaked foliage reaches waist-height a meter away from where they stand.

They drop their trousers without hesitation, revealing themselves to the stunned crowd before settling into a squatting position. From there, it's all downhill for them - awkwardly teetering on unsteady feet, they grab at each other to avoid collapse, but their balance won't hold. Like dominoes, they tumble backward into the soaking hedge.

The scene is chaotic - bodies sprawled everywhere among piss-drenched soil and gravel. Even the most hardened reveler cannot bear to look upon such depravity any longer, shielding his eyes with trembling hands as he tries not to take in more than his mind can stomach.

Moments later, they right themselves, hastily covering up before laughing together as they stagger back into the crowd and finally disappear into the night, ending what had been a fantastic evening with memories never to be forgotten and some that would haunt us.

Despite the chaos and debauchery, the night we had had been one of the most exhilarating experiences of my life. As we made our way back to the car, our ears still ringing from the incredible music, I couldn't help but feel a sense of awe at what we had just witnessed. Metallica had genuinely been at their best, and we had been a part of something magical.

As we drove away from the stadium, I couldn't help but glance back at the venue, still throbbing with energy. It was a night that I would never forget, a night that had changed me forever. And even though there had been moments of chaos and absurdity, those were just a tiny part of an unforgettable experience.

As we drove down the highway, the sounds of Metallica still rang in our ears, and from the car stereo, which was blasting the same songs repeatedly, my friends and I knew that we had just experienced something extraordinary. And they would stay with us for a lifetime.

Lasting memories with good friends Kim & Thor.

# Chapter 7

## Street Encounter

### 1994

As I walked down my local streets, I bumped into some people I knew and some I didn't; we were all getting along, but the atmosphere had something else in the air.

A short but ominous figure stepped out from the crowd, pulled out a small handgun, and pointed it around. When I challenged the gun's usefulness, he pointed it at me with icy cold eyes, challenging me if I dared to stand my ground. I could feel death looming on the horizon as if frozen in place until he suddenly lowered his weapon and shook my hand. It was then that an eternal bond of unexpected courage and sacrifice was sealed between us. That's how my closest friend and I became friends forever.

We continued walking down the street, my Heart still racing from the adrenaline. I couldn't believe this stranger had pointed a gun at me just moments ago, and now we were walking together as if nothing had happened. But there was something different about him now. He seemed almost relieved as if a heavy burden had been lifted from his shoulders.

As we walked, he began to open up to me. He told me about his struggles, fears, and what led him to that moment on the street. I listened intently, feeling a newfound empathy for him. It was as if the danger we had faced had somehow brought us together, allowing us to see each other in a new light.

∞ ∞ ∞

## Double Barrel Showdown

The drug dealer's unit door creaked open, and we burst inside, laughing maniacally after some beers. Our laughter died in our throats as we beheld the ominous sight of a side-by-side double-barrel shotgun pointed directly at us. The cold steel barrels were so close to my nose that I could feel its chill and see my breath fogging its surface. A menacing smile spread across the African dealer's face, his voice low and sharp: "Don't come rushing like that; I'm a little on edge tonight." With a sudden motion, he lowered the gun, and all was forgotten as he lit up the bong and smoked away.

I took a deep breath and tried to calm my rapidly beating Heart. The haze of the marijuana smoke swirled around us, mixing with the scent of sweat and fear. I watched as the drug dealer took another hit from the bong, his eyes closing in ecstasy as the smoke filled his lungs.

I knew staying here any longer was a dangerous game, but something profound inside me refused to back down. I walked towards the dealer, my hand reaching out to take the bong from him. His eyes met mine, and for a moment, I saw a flicker of something dark and predatory.

But then he smiled, his teeth gleaming in the dim light. "You've got balls, kid," he said, handing me the bong. "I like that. Maybe you and I can do business after all."

I took a hit from the bong, my mind buzzing with the adrenaline of the moment. I knew I was playing with fire, but I couldn't just sit and watch him smoke, and we didn't get any after that welcome.

The dealer grinned, revealing a row of yellowed teeth as I hit the bong and told us, "You guys are okay."

We left not long after as we had other places to visit, and we wanted to avoid hanging around if whoever he was expecting would turn up.

At the time, I had a strong relationship with a steady girlfriend I had been dating for several months. We moved into a large two-bedroom apartment with two kitchens, bathrooms, and a sizable living room. My best mate was already there, dating her friend. Things were going well: we worked full-time and spent our weekends partying and drinking.

It was a given that our youthful relationship would eventually end. Still, she decided to make it official on New Year's Eve when we attended a raucous party with our friends. I had no idea what to do; all my mates were smoking bongs and having a great time, so I figured 'the hell with it' and joined in.

I knew it was a bad idea the second I said yes, but my mouth moved faster than my brain.

I took my first bong head, and then 1 minute later, my insides churned, and my stomach twisted into knots as I stumbled to get outside, barely making it before I began to vomit.

Then, the broken relationship took over, and tears streamed down my cheeks as I headed for the path leading back home, humiliated at how easily I had been cut off. No matter how often I felt this pain, it hurt like hell.

As I walked, my mind raced with thoughts of her. Why did she have to do this on New Year's Eve? Why did she have to make a scene at the party? Couldn't she have done it privately? I felt like a fool for not seeing it coming. Had I been too blinded by love to notice the signs?

I stumbled down the dark, deserted streets, my mind still reeling from the breakup. The only sound was the crunch of the snow under my shoes. I didn't know where I was going, but I needed to get away from the party and the memories of her.

I stumbled back to our apartment, barely able to keep my balance, as I climbed the stairs. I fumbled with the keys as I reached the door, trying to get them in the lock. Finally,

I unlocked the door and stumbled inside, the room spinning around me. I collapsed onto the couch, tears streaming down my face as I tried to understand what had happened.

I learned in my later years that humans are brutal like that. However, I still stand by my moral code, and having ethics, treating people nicely, and being honest with them are worth more than anything so you can look at yourself in the mirror every day and know you are a good human.

We are here on this plane to learn a lesson. The Devil will try and give you an easy way out many times in life, but being honest, treating your friends and family the same as you would expect them, and always being truthful to their face means more than just running away and hiding from trouble. Face and deal with it, and you will sleep better at night. Being a good soul is more challenging work than being rude or inconsiderate, and it takes much more character and a more substantial human to be true to what is ethically the right way to treat people.

Not long after we signed the lease, the partying and apartment rent payments started to fall behind. We had no choice but to leave. I found another much cheaper place in a shared house with many other young people - it was an ideal situation as I only had to look out for myself and my one room.

This house wasn't ideal for getting back into the workforce or settling into everyday life, so relying on government assistance and selling marijuana became part of everyday life - alongside all the partying with everyone else.

I still played football regularly, but despite suffering, I loved the sport, so I would still not train as much as I should have. But then, I met a girl who will always be the one who got away. We hit it off immediately and started talking about everything under the sun.

I couldn't believe how easy it was to speak to her. She was different from any girl I had ever dated before. She was kind, compassionate, and had a heart of gold. She didn't judge me for my past mistakes.

Her friends were not so welcoming; their jealousy had gotten in the way. One night, my supposed friend stayed at my place and then spread rumors that I had slept with her when nothing happened. I was too naive to realize what was happening until months later when they stopped coming around.

Also, at this time in my life, I had no goal, and hanging out with friends and smoking Hash was the way of life.

The small town felt like a trap; the only option was to get stuck in a dead-end job with no hope of escape. I remember our teacher asking us what we wanted to do after graduating. I'd declared that I wanted to be a fighter jet pilot like Tom Cruise, and the teacher had let out a scoff of disbelief as she looked at my grades. I was taken aback, feeling embarrassed and angry for never having been given the chance or support to achieve my dream. It only made me more determined to look elsewhere for any future possibilities.

When the year ended, I had a solid A- average - not great, but not bad. By then, I was set on a different path than most of my peers, one that did not involve a conventional 9 to 5 job and ownership of a Villa, Volvo, and Woof dog. My friends were my whole world, and that was all that mattered to me. We spent our days lounging around, smoking weed, and discussing our plans that never seemed to materialize. We were happy just living in the moment.

# Chapter 8

## Roskilde Festival

### 1995

My first Roskilde Festival experience was an unforgettable one. It was full of mischievous activities, from smoking a Turkish water pipe to brushing my teeth with beer.

The music festival ran from Monday to Sunday, and musicians kicked off their performances on Wednesday. When we arrived on the first day, thousands of people were queuing up to get in.

After successfully joining the merry chaos, our group settled down and pitched tents close together to form a circle for a bonfire and some privacy. We built the pipe, as mentioned earlier, and used it to smoke weed, which provided us with hours of entertainment and giggles.

As the days went by, the festival and we grew wilder. We were partying all day and all night, barely getting any sleep. The music was so loud that even our tents were vibrating. It was exhilarating and exhausting all at the same time.

As the sun began to set and the sky turned a beautiful shade of orange, we could hear the distant sounds of music coming from the festival grounds. We decided to make our way over and join the crowd. Inside the festival, the atmosphere was electric. People were dancing, jumping, and singing along to the music. We went from one stage to another, enjoying every genre of music we could find. As the night wore on, we found ourselves at an electronic music stage. The bass was so loud it shook the ground beneath us. We danced until our legs gave out, and our bodies were drenched in sweat. After the music ended, we returned to our tents, drained yet excited about the day's events. I noticed a girl in a tent nearby, struggling to set up her tent in the dark.

I went over to help her, and we struck up a conversation. Her name was Lily, and she was camping alone. We talked for hours, shared a joint before the night ended, and enjoyed a quiet smoke with a beautiful, friendly stranger.

During this time, we sat at one of the T-sections near the tent area, in full view of everyone around us. It got the attention of passersby and granted us many opportunities to socialize.

In a moment of clarity, I had the brilliant thought to write signs in English that read, "Show us your tits." The idea was that no one would know who we were since we were foreigners and thus wouldn't face any repercussions for their actions. We also created arrows pointing towards our sign so people would be sure to find it. Surprisingly, this worked like a charm, and the ladies we encountered delighted us many times during the afternoon by showing us what they had.

The funniest moment was when some guys appeared and began complaining that it wouldn't work, and right then, a girl took her shirt off next to them. They stood there with their mouths agape before turning around and wanting to join us. However, we kindly informed them that it wasn't working, so they should go elsewhere.

As the sun set, my friends and I stumbled drunkenly back to our tents, laughing about the day's events. We couldn't believe how easy it was for women to show us their breasts. It was like we had the magic touch. The air was thick with the scent of sex and sweat, making my Heart race excitedly.

As we entered our campsite, I threw myself onto the sleeping bag, exhausted yet satisfied.

My friend sat beside me, a look of contentment on his face. "That was insane," he said, his voice still hoarse from all the shouting.

I chuckled. "Yeah, it was. I can't believe it worked."

He grinned. "I told you it would. You have to know how to play the game."

I nodded in agreement. Michael was always the smooth talker who knew what to say to get what he wanted. I admired him for it, envied him even.

We sat silently, listening to the bonfire sounds before having a last beer and bong before bed.

Every morning, we would brush our teeth with beer because there was no access to water, then have a suck on the shisha and lay in the sun until midday when the music and the adventures began.

Two guys stumbled upon our camp one afternoon, claiming that the Turkish water pipe we had built was utter crap and only a tourist souvenir. We offered them a go on it anyway – warning them that it could create quite a bit of smoke without much avail – and the first guy decided to take us up. When he exhaled, he stumbled backward and crashed right through the side of a tent, with clouds of smoke billowing out of him from standing straight up to lying flat on the ground. We all cheered and laughed like Nelson from The Simpsons, pointing at his helplessness as he attempted to stand but couldn't. His mate had to pull him away after multiple failed attempts. Later that day, they returned asking if they could borrow our pipe, which was met with an adamant "No" from everyone present. After all, it was just a shitty tourist souvenir. But we did lend them one of our most diminutive and embarrassing pipes; they left with disgusted looks on their faces and a few jibes in tow.

The bands I had been watching throughout the night were a mix of old-school and hardcore:

- Ice T's intense rhymes.
- Body Count's unbridled Rage.
- The Cranberries' melancholic tunes.
- The Offspring's street punk vibes.
- Konkhra's death metal screams.
- Biohazard's breakneck rhythms.

- Napalm Death's shock-rock energy.

But then it happened. Someone screamed in my face as we stood close to the stage during The Cranberries' set. Instinct took over as his fist swung towards me, too close for me to raise my hands in time. Desperate, I reached out and grabbed his shirt instead, tugging him into a headbutt before he disappeared from view. Around me, I spotted several of what I assumed were his friends closing in. I ducked and scrambled through the crowd without hesitation until I found my mate by the hot dog stand. Quickly, I yelled at him to leave; neither questioning nor protesting, we instantly melted away into the crowd and escaped.

We knew it was time to return to reality as the festival ended. We packed up our tents and said our goodbyes to the new friends we had made, including Lily, who had become a close companion during the five days we spent at Roskilde.

As we drove away, I couldn't help but feel a sense of sadness. The festival was an unforgettable experience that allowed us to let loose and be free. Still, now it was over. As we returned to our everyday lives, I knew that the memories of Roskilde would stay with me forever.

As the car drove off into the distance, I closed my eyes. I took a deep breath and reminisced about the week behind me.I don't think I woke up until the car stopped at my house before I pulled my camping gear out of the boot and walked inside, and it all just felt like a dream.

We went again the following year, 1996, and the leading bands we experienced were The Sex Pistol Come Back, Sepultura, Slayer, Rage Against the Machine, Cypress Hill & Red Hot Chili Peppers.

The craziest lineup ever

Let's start with the headliners:

- David Bowie
- Nick Cave & the Bad Seeds
- Björk
- Red Hot Chili Peppers
- Neil Young & Crazy Horse

- Patti Smith
- But wait! There's also the fine print:
- Rage Against the Machine
- Cypress Hill
- Massive Attack
- Foo Fighters
- Alanis Morissette
- Dave Matthews Band
- No Doubt
- Sepultura
- Slayer
- Pulp
- The Cocteau Twins
- Frank Black
- Bad Religion
- Billy Bragg
- Flaming Lips
- Frontline Assembly
- Pop Will Eat Itself
- Presidents of the United States of America
- Type O Negative
- Toots & the Maytals
- Underworld
- Ministry

At the time, I had a job at a factory that manufactured kombi campers and no holidays to take. So, I took a week off unofficially; I called in sick.

Of course, this decision ended up on the national newspaper's front page when we attended the Sepultura concert.

Even though it wasn't a big picture of me alone, I could tell the manager had knowledge of our outing and talked about the festival for weeks afterward, which made for many uncomfortable discussions about festival life and how he always had wanted to go but never had the chance.

But as I stood in that crowd, surrounded by thousands of other music lovers, I felt it was exactly where I was meant to be. The festival's energy was infectious, and I couldn't help but get swept up in the music.

I remember standing in the front row for Rage Against the Machine, feeling the bass reverberate through my chest as I screamed along with the lyrics. Nothing else mattered at that moment except for the music and the connection I felt with everyone around me.

And then there was Björk - her ethereal voice and avant-garde performance sending shivers down my spine. I felt like I was witnessing something truly magical and unique.

But it wasn't just the headliners that left an impression on me. I discovered new bands and artists I would never have listened to, like Massive Attack and Alanis Morissette. I danced like crazy to Cypress Hill and Underworld and screamed.

The Sex Pistols' return to the stage was an incredible event--but it only lasted about eighteen minutes before they stormed off, with some people throwing bottles at them. It was whispered that they were too aged and out of shape to put on a whole show, so they planned the early exit to maintain their Punk Rock personas without appearing inept.

## Fly's, Bongs & Freedom

One midday stands out in my mind. We were a group of about ten people, puffing away on bongs and enjoying the freedom of our festival-like atmosphere. Even one of the guys who didn't usually smoke was hitting the bong hard. My friend and I captured a fly between two pieces of polystyrene. We cut a couple of slits into each cup and then blew smoke from the bong head through them to get the fly "in a festival mood." To our surprise, This worked much better than expected, as when we released it, the fly was so slow that my friend could catch it with his hand multiple times, leaving us all in hysterics.

Of course, we weren't much better off than the little bug, and after a few minutes, it managed to escape.

The person mentioned above, Sören, was sitting outside our tent, and the fly flew past his face before it hit the top of a tent pole next to him.

He described that as resulting in the fly doing several somersaults before landing on its back on the tent lining, where it slid a full meter before flipping over again and taking off in a zigzag pattern.

I couldn't help but chuckle at the thought of the clumsy fly. It reminded me of myself, stumbling and tripping through life without much grace.

We can all agree that in the 90s, some fantastic hashish could be found in Denmark. That year's Roskilde festival was the perfect place to indulge. The unmistakable scent of weed filled the air everywhere we went, and it seemed like everyone was smoking something.

But it wasn't just the weed that made that year's festival unforgettable. Every band that performed gave it their all, and the energy of the crowds was electric. The mosh pits never stopped, and the air was thick with sweat and adrenaline.

One of the festival's most memorable moments was during the Rage Against the Machine set. As they launched into "Killing in the Name," the crowd surged forward, creating a massive pit that seemed to go on forever. I found myself caught up in the crowd, bouncing off of bodies and screaming the lyrics along with everyone else.

It was pure chaos, but it was also incredibly exhilarating. For those few minutes, I felt like I was part of something larger than myself, something that transcended the usual boundaries. I never did see Lily again after that year's festival, but the memories of that week still lingered in my mind, and I knew that I would always hold those moments close to my Heart.

As the years went by, I attended many more festivals and concerts, but none could match the magic of Roskilde in the 90s.

The sense of freedom, the camaraderie, the music, the drugs, and the debauchery made it an unforgettable experience that I will always cherish.

Looking back at it now, I couldn't help but feel nostalgic for those wild and carefree days. The world has changed so much since then, and things will never be quite the same. But every time I hear those old punk and metal anthems, I am transported back to that time and place, and I feel young again, with my whole life ahead of me.

Those festivals were a rite of passage for me and many others lucky to attend.

## Test Bombings

Throughout the years, I got mixed up with some unsavory characters, and one of them offered me a nice profit if I helped him resell illegal fireworks. These were some heavy-duty firecrackers known as "Signal Firecrackers." Young people like me highly sought after them, but I wasn't in it to sell them; I just wanted to set them off.

One night, I was meeting two brothers. The younger brother wanted to do a test bombing. "this was a reference to France doing Nuclear test bombings at the time" on an old fridge they had outside, so we lugged it down the stairs from the first floor and placed it about 30 meters away. After lighting the fuse, my "bomb technician" closed the door quickly before we hurried back. As soon as the door shut, you could hear the suction from inside because the firecracker had sucked out all the air. Then came an almighty bang, and the next thing we saw was the fridge flipping onto its back from the explosion and shooting its door high into the air, which ended with a loud metal thud when it hit the ground. We laughed like little kids and inspected the now-dented refrigerator with round sides instead of square ones. We threw it aside and went upstairs to tell our story.

As a reckless teenager, I decided to grab a bite to eat at the local grill bar down the street. Being paranoid about potentially encountering the police, I armed myself with only one extra signal cracker. I stashed my hold box of twenty somewhere safe. As I approached the grill, I noticed a tunnel running through the buildings next door. I threw the remaining flash bang into it before quickly entering the restaurant. The girl behind the counter jumped when she heard the explosion but laughed when she realized it was just me.

Not long after, police officers stormed into the grill bar and demanded that I explain what had happened. I told them I had been inside when the explosion occurred and wasn't sure what had caused it. Luckily, the girl behind the counter verified my story and confirmed that I was inside when it went off. After searching me and finding nothing suspicious about my person, the officers reluctantly left and looked elsewhere for answers.

I thanked my friend for always having my back before leaving with my food and disappearing into the night to avoid causing more trouble for the locals.

## Bad Company

The primary weed dealer in our town was infamous for giving people credit for their purchases. He had a scheme where he would give his customers tick; "Credit" and wait outside the local bank every Friday when benefits were paid out. It was only the one bank where this took place. On his way to the bank early in the morning, he would take a hit and grab his nun chucks, knife, and gun before hopping on his moped. He'd also bring a six-pack of beer and sit outside the bank collecting what people owed him all day.

Folks who strolled by grumbled that this faction of people were being obnoxious, swigging drinks and lounging around the bank. Some even stopped in to pay or negotiate another deal; others tried to rat out their comrades to try and get a reward or special rate. Though these spectators did not approve of his profession, he was more than likely earning more money than most of them without them having any knowledge.

I recall when I visited his house, and his mates laughed as I arrived. He was holding a blood-stained tea towel to his head. He had been showing off his 22 caliber, cut down from a rifle size into a small handgun, so it didn't offer much damage. When demonstrating it, the bullet ricocheted off his motorcycle helmet. It hit him in between the eyebrows, staying lodged an inch beneath the skin further up. He then squeezed out the bullet like a pimple and used whiskey to disinfect it. To calm himself down, he smoked a bong, the thick smoke filling the small, dimly lit room.

I couldn't help but feel uneasy as I sat on the raggedy couch, the smell of weed and whiskey mixing in the air. The friends seemed unfazed by the incident, cracking jokes and passing around joints. But I couldn't shake off the feeling that I was in the company of unpredictable people.

As the night wore on, I listened as they talked about their latest deals and run-ins with the law. One guy boasted about getting away with assault by bribing the cops. At the same time, another talked about how he had threatened a rival dealer with a machete afterward.

The most horrifying story was when they got into heavy drug use.

One night, when his best friend was around and had fallen asleep, he and his girlfriend decided to play a prank on him while he was sleeping: they thought it would be funny to paint his face with a marker, give him sunglasses, and draw a beard on him.

The situation then spiraled out of control; they removed his clothes and poured ketchup all over his body.

Unfortunately, he had overdosed and was already dead by this point. When the paramedics and police arrived, they found a corpse covered in ketchup and his face painted.

And this didn't look good for anyone involved.

No one from the group is around anymore. Sadly, their drug addiction had taken complete hold of them and taken them too soon without them ever getting the chance for a somewhat normal life.

I couldn't help but feel a chill run down my spine as I left that house. These were not the kind of people you wanted to be associated with, yet I was drawn to their story. Their dangerous lifestyle was thrilling and captivating, but it also came with a price. I realized then that I needed to stay away from these kinds of people, lest I end up like them - dead and forgotten.

As I walked down the dark street, I could hear the distant sounds of police sirens and the raucous laughter of my former acquaintances. I knew that I was lucky to have gotten out when I did, but I also knew that others were not as fortunate. The lure of drugs and easy money was too strong for some, and they would continue to fall prey to the seductive call of the wrong company that I had left behind. It was a sobering thought but one that I couldn't ignore.

Years have passed since that fateful night at the weed dealer's house, but the memory of it still lingers. I can't help but wonder what could have been if they had chosen a different path in life.

As I sit in my living room, sipping on a glass of whiskey, I can't help but feel grateful for the life I have chosen. Sure, it may not be as exciting or profitable as dealing drugs, but at least I won't end up like those poor souls who let addiction consume them.

I take a deep breath and sigh in relief as I think about the people I have in my life. My Wife, who supports me in everything I do, and the friends I can always count on for help.

## A Fresh Start

I had relocated to my dad's house to distance myself from my hometown and the drugs that was consuming it. After a few months, I met a girl at a bar one night, and we hit it off. We started to see each other regularly when our schedules allowed, and I was employed at a large factory in Copenhagen with my father as its director.

He got me a job to lend a helping hand with the expansion of the business, which included setting up offices and moving around stock. I was eventually permanently stationed at the stock supplies end and asked to help elsewhere when needed. The main product we sold was revolving doors for large shopping centers across the globe; many orders were from Middle Eastern countries, who had the money to pay for luxury items like that. I immensely enjoyed working there, partly due to my excellent relationship with the staff, particularly my stock manager, who taught me a lot about providing and managing stock internationally.

After close to a year of hard work, my dad urged my girlfriend and me to look into investing in an apartment. Owning our place would be unique, and the investment would have a strong future. So, for the next month or so, we searched for options and talked to the bank. Eventually, we stumbled across the perfect spot close to my job and agreed that this was it.

As the day approached that I was due to get a ride home from work with my father, anticipation of signing the documents for our dream property surged. My dad would be the guarantor for the bank, as is typical for first-time buyers needing surety.

On the drive home, I reminded him about the meeting at the bank, and his response rocked me to my core - "What do you mean?" He had never agreed to sign any paperwork! Stunned silence filled the car as I attempted to process what he said. Nothing we had worked so hard for was a reality. After all these months of planning, it felt like a joke.

But this didn't feel funny. This felt like a betrayal, and no words could express the shock and hurt I felt when it came from my father.

For the remainder of the journey home, I was silent. When I arrived, I called my girlfriend and relayed what had happened. I then asked her dad if he would be willing to come to collect me and help me move my belongings; I could no longer stay there after the incident. He agreed, and within an hour, we had loaded all my things into his van, and I had left my father's house without fully comprehending what had transpired. This occurrence put a definitive end to my relationship with him and my younger brothers who lived with him; they were only told that I had gone, so they felt abandoned and betrayed by me. Sadly, this is still true today - it has been over twenty five years since this event, but I still do not have any actual contact with them.

After moving my belongings to my girlfriend's house, our relationship couldn't sustain the strain, and I was back in my small town with no clear future. Drugs quickly began to retake control of my life and drinking and smoking became a way of masking the personal issues I had been trying to ignore. I was still in love with her, but staying when I had nothing to offer didn't make sense. I quickly fell back into my old lifestyle: meeting up with friends, smoking, and drinking. Every day felt like party time until the future became foreseeable again.

I don't blame my dad for this now, but the hurt at the time was real and changed the course of my direction in life. But as they say, what doesn't kill you only makes you stronger.

This definitely taught me how to bring up my kids in a safe and loving environment where they have both a mum and a dad to help them learn how to operate through life and that they have the correct morals and ethics to be successful in life and as a good human being.

∞∞∞

## *Skiing in Val-D'isere*

In an attempt to start over and take back control of my future, I joined a Sports School with a friend of mine. This School taught skiing, and we would visit France each month for two weeks.

I used this opportunity to get back into shape, running daily in preparation for our upcoming ski trips. This change was perfect for me: I returned to a healthy routine and balanced diet that facilitated my training. We were taken on a bus ride across Europe, ending in Val-D'isere in the French Alps.

The drive to the French town was an adventure, but it tested our patience.

Life there was laid-back, and we appreciated being able to purchase cans of Coca-Cola, which back home was outlawed. My skiing skills improved rapidly, and I adored it more than I imagined. Before the ski season started, the mountains retained a layer of snow since they were located on a glacier so that you could ski year-round. Additionally, it was typically thirty degrees, and you could get a tan while skiing shirtless.

The sudden change from hot to cold is shocking when you walk through the streets of town and then move into the shade of a building; the temperature can quickly drop from 30°C to almost freezing. You'll be sure to seek out the sun once again!

It's amusing when entering stores in France or waiting for ski lift lines because there is no implied etiquette that people should line up one after another and patiently await their turn.

Unlike in some other countries, France does not have a queue culture, meaning there is no unspoken rule about standing behind one another and waiting your turn to move up in a line. If someone sees an opening, they will take it immediately - without feeling the need to apologize or express guilt for "cutting" in front of someone else. It may take some adjustment, and you must get used to this behavior.

The younger French skiers would zoom down the slope and stop abruptly to slide into one of the queues. They'd try to get as far ahead as possible while waiting at the ski lift with 100 other people. Another trick they would pull was to insert their ski pole into the locking mechanism on your ski. As soon as the line started moving, they would press down hard to release your foot from its binding. Then, before you had a chance to regain your balance, they'd quickly sneak past you laughing.

When you're visiting the Alps, toilets are a bit different. The plumbing is usually weaker compared to other places, so it isn't recommended to flush toilet paper after wiping. So you should put it into a bin or receptacle near the toilet to avoid clogging and causing problems for the entire hotel. On the plus side, the views and air quality can be amazing! You feel free, and life moves slower without the city hustle and bustle. It's a unique way of living, and I was grateful for the change.

As my skiing skills continued improving, I became more adventurous. One day, I decided to venture off the beaten path and explore some of the more remote areas of the mountain. The thrill of carving through the fresh powder, with nothing but the sound of the wind and my breath filling my ears, was unlike anything I had ever experienced.

We usually put lots of energy into partying at the hotel bar on Friday and Saturday evenings. We would sleep off our hangovers on Sunday before hitting the slopes again on Monday. It was an intriguing experience since most people who ski in Denmark are wealthy or upper middle class. At the resort, I was one of a handful of skiers from the poorer part of society, making for some clashes between different types of people – which meant I wasn't particularly popular with the wealthier males who felt they were better than us. I didn't let their attitude get to me, though. After all, I was there to ski and have fun, not to make friends with snobby rich guys. On the other hand, my friend seemed to enjoy their company and would often disappear with them to the hotel bar after a day on the slopes.

One night, we were all out drinking, and I went to the restroom, leaving my cigarettes and lighter on the table. When I returned, they had vanished, and nobody at the same table knew what happened. A couple of weeks later, we were on a bus, and something fell out of the pocket of the person in front of me. It was my lighter—the same one I'd bought at that specialty store before our trip to France. Everyone recognized it as mine; his expression when I pointed it out was priceless, and the thief was exposed. He tried to play it off as a mistake, but I could tell he was guilty. I decided to let it go, though, instead focused my energy on skiing and enjoying the rest of my trip.

The course ended early due to an upcoming slalom competition I had trained hard for. As the poorest person in the group, I had added to the lowest level, so I knew my chances of moving up were slim. However, I knew I could show the higher-ups that they could be beaten with my natural talent in the slalom event. On the test day, I was told the wrong departure time and had to rush to the kitchen staff, which were also going up the mountain. Thankfully, the chef agreed to take me and only made me 20 minutes late.

When I sprinted to the starting point, one of the teachers told me I was too late and would not be allowed to join in the friendly competition. I argued that it wasn't fair since they had yet to start, reminding her that a Höjskole is a place for all types of people to come together and have a good time. But my efforts were in vain. Then, I realized I did not belong with them and would probably never get their respect. So, I turned around and left. Skiing back to the restaurant where I could take the underground train to the valley, As I descended the mountain, my mind was filled with a mix of disappointment and anger. I felt like I had wasted all my time and effort trying to prove myself to these people who looked down on me. I realized I didn't need their validation to feel good about myself. I had already achieved so much just by being able to experience the thrill of skiing and the beauty of the Alps.

The next day, we took the bus ride home.

That same night, we returned to Denmark, and I headed on the long voyage back to our hometown. After two days of travel by bus, I took another five hours to reach home via ferry and two trains. When I finally arrived and reconnected with my real friends, the scars of my father's betrayal still lingered in my mind. It was difficult, if not impossible, for me to forgive him, and that pain resurfaced every time I faced similar situations.

∞∞∞∞

## Drug Den Danger

Spending time most days at a known weed dealer's house, they always made for weird and crazy things to happen.

This day quickly turned from sitting around on the floor smoking weed and playing PC games running a 150mHz processor and Duke-Nukem, which at the time was high-tech.

During my visits to the dealer's house, I had grown accustomed to the weird and crazy antics that came with it. But on this day, things took an unexpected turn.

Another dealer was soon to arrive with backup and a loaded weapon in tow due to unfinished business about an electric guitar deal, etc.

Three hurried to the front door, two with firearms and one with a large bowie knife. Meanwhile, I and some others kept watch from different windows upstairs. I was the first to spot them when they parked: two men and a baby strapped into a car seat in the back were inside. I warned everyone that they weren't alone —they had a child with them.

This only made everyone more agitated. The knife-wielding guy ran straight towards the car, and the pistol-wielder had taken cover by the front door, aiming directly at the vehicle. This made the two occupants reconsider their position, and one emerged, making excuses for why they were there. After a short moment, they decided it was best to leave and departed shortly after that. I remember the armed guy got arrested sometime later for starting 18-plus fights with more than 20 victims in one evening, drugged up and going crazy.

The knife-wielding guy got jailed some months later for a bank robbery he committed after owing money to some bikers after he had avoided paying them back for some time.

The henchmen forced the knife guy into the back of a car, driving deep into a nearby forest. He was handed a shovel and told to start digging his grave with a shovel they threw at him. - Unless he paid off his debt in full.

He pleaded with them, and they gave him one last chance. They parked down the street from a bank and tossed him a bag and a gun. Knowing it was his only chance for survival, he entered the building and demanded money. As he ran out with the cash, sirens blared in the distance, quickly gaining on him. His instructions were to run past the car and throw the money bag into it before continuing.

Passersby screamed as they caught sight of him, but he kept running, knowing if he stopped now, it would be over. He had to get away or risk being stuffed in that same carboot for burial. Seeing the car parked as instructed, the henchmen waited for him. Running past the vehicle, he quickly threw the money bag inside and continued down the road.

The sirens were getting louder and closer, and he knew he had to find a way to lose them. He saw a nearby alley and quickly turned down it, hoping to find a way out. However, as he descended the narrow path, he realized it was a dead end.

He could hear the sirens coming closer and the sound of police officers shouting commands at him. He knew he had to get on his knees and take the coming punishment, which was better than being buried back in the woods where he had dug his grave.

∞∞∞

## Gun Point Dread

Walking down the main street in my home village, I spot a ragged junkie with sunken eyes and scabbed skin shuffling towards me. Before I can react, he locks eyes with me and yanks out a gleaming nine-millimeter from his pocket. Panic surges through me as I realize we are only ten meters apart. I freeze, staring down the gun barrel, trying to comprehend what he wants from me.

With a sudden jerk, I throw my arms to the side, shouting, "What do you want?!" But my voice barely carries over the sound of my Heart thudding in my chest. The junkie pulls the trigger, but nothing happens - it's a dud. Cursing under his breath, he tries to un-jam the weapon by repeatedly pulling back on the slide.

We are all locked in a deadly dance at that moment - me and this crazed man wielding a broken gun. We stare at each other, frozen in terror, until a burst of adrenaline sends us all scrambling for safety. Heart pounding and breaths coming in short gasps, I haul ass around the corner of a tunnel with just one thought in mind - getting away.

# Chapter 9

## The Lioness Den & A Rude Awakening

### 1996

We were determined to go on a weekend excursion together, me and my best friend.

He drove his glistening raised US Army Willy Jeep - all black with massive wheels, nothing more than a windshield and roll cage between us and the summer weather.

Our destination? Helsingör is a coastal city in Denmark where we planned to camp on the beach.

He casually mentioned that he would also catch up with his ex-girlfriend, who was now dating a patched biker who had previously tried to shoot him. But he assured me it was all sorted now. I nodded hesitantly, unsure of what lay ahead.

The mood in the car was charged with anticipation. As we made it closer to our destination, we read in the newspaper and heard on the radio that the president of a local Biker chapter had been killed that week, gunned down by a sniper while driving his Harley. An eerie silence spread through the car until our destination came into view, like a reminder of death looming over us.

This was when we had cell phones, but their service and reception could have been better, and there wasn't any internet access. All they were good for were texts and calls.

My friend had organized to meet her at the apartment on the cell phone while her boyfriend was away so that it would be easy.

This may lead to drama, but I couldn't do anything about that now.

We got to the area in a housing project – large apartment complexes with two staircases per building leading up to 12 apartments on either side.

We met with the girl who welcomed us into her home, alone since her biker boyfriend was at work.

We leave there within an hour and arrange to meet her on the beach later that afternoon.

And, of course, the boyfriend finds out and wants to join in with a few friends.

So we are at the beach now, the 2 of us, three bikers, and the ex-girlfriend.

It works out fine between the initial interrogation and everyone being relaxed and then deciding to return to their place to drink beers after the beach.

The evening goes fine with a few paranoid moments, the main one being when we run out of beers and the Biker wants my friend and him to drive alone down to get some more, and he is pretty adamant that I can wait there with the others while they are away.

It was a tense 30 minutes before they came back, but everything turned out fine, and we left around midnight, drunk and ready to sleep.

We veered off the main highway and onto the beach, parking our car at the edge of the sand and tall grass. We set up camp so that when the tide arrived, it wouldn't reach us before smoking a joint and drinking another beer as we relaxed into bedtime.

I was abruptly awakened by someone shaking my foot, still in the sleeping bag, wearing shoes as it had gotten cold overnight. I thought my friend was trying to wake me, but when I opened my eyes, it was a full-grown fox biting and shaking my foot. After screaming out loud, the fox ran away. At the same time, my companion woke up, checked if I was okay, and then dismissed my story of an animal attack—saying I was just drunk and stoned—before telling me to go back to sleep.

I was about to drift off again when I heard my friend scream like a small child; upon looking up, I saw the fox standing straight on his chest and staring him in the eyes. At the sound of a second scream (loud enough to scare away evil spirits), the fox ran off, and we chased after it, throwing bottles at it before giving up. Opting for safety over comfort, we spent the rest of the night in our car, cramped together around the handbrake and me lying in the metal tray behind the front seats. It wasn't comfortable, but at least it was safe from foxes, and soon enough, we both fell asleep.

I slowly came to around 8:30 a.m., feeling pain all over from sleeping in the back of an ute. It was already sweltering outside, with temperatures hovering near 30 degrees Celsius. We were parked on the beach, and tracks in the sand indicated how we ended up there.

As I stand up to stretch and start looking around for what's going on, I realize I'm in my boxer shorts at the top of a raised black Willy Jeep Ute, surrounded by hundreds of people on a packed beach, kids playing in the sand and families having a great time, seeing them staring at me, I quickly scramble to put on my camo shorts before waking my friend up and yelling that we needed to leave immediately.

We packed up quickly and excused ourselves to the families who had to move out of the way for us to drive the truck out from the beach while spinning up sand in the process before we were on our way home, laughing at the weekend craziness and what adventure would come next. While driving home, we talked about the weekend's events and couldn't believe the crazy situations we had found ourselves in. My friend laughed and said, "I don't think I've ever had a weekend like that." I chuckled in agreement and replied, "Yeah, I don't think we'll forget this one anytime soon."

# Chapter 10

## Train Ride On The Edge

### 1997

We occasionally take the train and plan to smoke during this time.

Usually, this would involve a 500ml Coke bottle bong with a green garden hose attachment and an aluminum foil bong head that could be filled and lifted as needed.

We were six friends going to Copenhagen, which would involve a 1-hour train ride, and part of that we would be seated in a six-person coupe with sliding doors entry and curtains.

We were heading to a Metallica concert, and the atmosphere was electric.

The coupe had a big window where the top half could be pulled down to get airflow in, but it was also perfect for blowing smoke out just near the edge when the window was just opened slightly (if you know, you know)

So, it is the perfect scenario for travel and smoking bongs simultaneously.

Everything was going perfectly. The conductor had checked our tickets, so he shouldn't be coming back when he can see it's still us.

Curtains are drawn closed, and we are passing the bong around, and obviously, several stories are going on and shit going down.

As we passed around the bong, the train began to pick up speed, and we could feel the rumble of the tracks beneath us. The excitement of the Metallica concert was palpable, and we were all eager to arrive in Copenhagen and let loose.

And then suddenly, mid-conversation, one of the guys (let's call him Anders) looks at the bong head and pulls it out from the bong like it's his turn!

But it wasn't; Christian was mid-suck to finish a head, resulting in full backflow. Just imagine mouth-to-bong suction reversed. We got more smoke than we ever wanted or needed to be blown straight out into the coupe as the head gets lifted. By now, he sucks up most of the bong water, which had been pretty abused, brown and vile juicy liquid.

He starts coughing, chucking smoke, and bits of weed/ tobacco are coming out of him, and he is about to find the highest high!

Meanwhile, our friend Rune has hit panic mode and is running around shouting, "Oh no, we are fucked! Oh no, we will get arrested! Oh no, someone do something!" Meanwhile, everyone else laughed or tried to avoid getting hit by spewing and bong water and loved the situation.

We lunged into another free coupe, the adrenaline coursing through our veins. Everything was fine, although the atmosphere was still buzzing, and Rune took a while to settle down from his panic attack.

As we settled into our new compartment, we couldn't help but laugh at the situation's absurdity. The smell of smoke and bong water lingered in the air, but we didn't care. We were young and reckless, and nothing could stop us.

The rest of the journey passed in a blur of smoke and excitement. We chatted and joked and listened to music, all the while watching the world rush by outside the window. The closer we got to Copenhagen, the more our anticipation grew.

We were all buzzing with energy and excitement when we finally arrived at the station. We stumbled off the train, giggling and joking with each other.

## *Surprise Butt Attack*

Mid-afternoon, several of us younger players visited one of the older players, who was maybe ten years older, and a local biker (let's call him Kaj) who had been through the darker corners of life. Still, he was outlandish and always got super excited when we drank. It started with us sitting around the lounge room's coffee table, drinking cheap beers and talking soccer.

After a few beers, when the atmosphere is high and the music is playing, one of the younger lads comes out of the toilet and, for a laugh, shouts, "Check this out." When everyone turns around, he moons us all and laughs triumphantly.

*" Mooning* is displaying one's bare buttocks by removing clothing, e.g., by lowering the backside of one's trousers and underpants, usually bending over." Kaj quickly shouts, "Do that again."

As I know now, If someone calls that out to you, Then never do it! So he does, and as he has stuck the moon in our faces this time, Kaj, in one swift move with no spit "that I know of," has poked his finger into the butthole up to the second knuckle. I saw the attack from the side view, and my friend looked directly at us; the face told it all as he wrenches over like one should after such an attack. He whimpers lightly and jumps away, trying to get his pants on. At the same time, Kaj smelled the finger and pronounced loudly and proudly, "Wow," THAT'S A GOOD ONE, then turned to the person next to him and gave him a Dirty Sanchez wipe. He then starts gagging and chucking up and running for the sink.

*"Dirty Sanchez" After anal sex, the act of drawing a mustache on the recipient's face with the object of penetration*

Another friend and I have collapsed on the floor, sliding off the couch laughing. Kaj walks to the kitchen, and I hear him washing his hands, opening the fridge, and getting a fresh beer.

I can hear the distinctive POP from the bottle cap being opened with a lighter, and Kaj returns to the living room, taking a swig of the beer. Then, he looks at us on the ground, still laughing,

and then asks, "What are you guys laughing at?"
Like that's old news, he just anally penetrated our friend in front of us, and what happened since then only made everyone laugh harder.
More beers were opened, more people arrived, more beers were drunk, and the tale of the Dirty Sanchez was born.

∞∞∞

## From Drunk To Stoned In His Sleep

On an ordinary evening, my best mate and I were having a ball, just smoking Bongs and engaging in silly behavior, when another friend of ours turned up. He had been out drinking and was pretty smashed by then, so we had a quick chat, and he retreated to another room to sleep.
Not long after, he was fast asleep and snoring loudly throughout the shared rooms where we were staying.
Without missing a beat, my friend packed a huge bong head and told me to follow him and be quiet.
So we sneak into the room where the sleeping person is, and my mate lights the bong, inhales the entire thing, and holds it until the exact time the snoring starts. He gently blows the whole content of the smoke into the nostrils, and then we wait.
Now let's just recap as this was a head that would put any average person down to their knees, and this guy just smoked it with his nose, without knowing, and drunk.
A few seconds pass, and then the coughing starts; he wakes up and coughs while smoke comes out simultaneously. I'm sure I can see his eyes reddening as this happens and the confusion on his face as he knows he fell asleep drunk, but now he is stoned and coughing smoke out.
We are now rolling on the floor in stitches, and our friend is more confused and angry, but he can't fight us because he isn't

cable, and it's funny, especially when you have been smoking.

We then retreat into our room and let him be to get a good night's sleep while having a long laugh about his look when he woke up and smoke coming out of him like an angry Dragon, not knowing what hit him.

∞ ∞ ∞

## A Dark Encounter With A Giant

One thing I remember from my teenage years was the Hoo Hoo Man.

He was a local legend, and many kids were terrified of him as he would be seen around the area.

The Hoo Hoo Guy, standing at an impressive 6 foot 4, had strawberry-blonde hair and a scruffy beard. His teeth were slightly crooked. He'd wander around the neighborhood silently and suddenly make this loud hoo-hoo noise when he noticed someone nearby — which often frightened people!

This would scare most people, and as he would almost sneak up on you and then, not having a personal space filter, he would get very close to your face, and then he would raise his hand to wave hello and make these sounds hoo hoo.

He was a harmless human being, and there was no ill intention. Still, he had grown up with this condition and could not communicate with people, and all he knew was to smile and make this sound.

His parents lived close to where we had for years, so we'd see him often. But on dark nights, it was still startling when we'd hear HOO HOO HOO from somewhere in the shadows close by, and it felt like every time we stepped outside, his haunting HOO HOO HOO was waiting for us. Then suddenly, he'd emerge from the darkness, a towering figure with an eerie smile and enormous teeth glinting in the moonlight that sent chills down our spine. Even knowing he was just a friendly person with no ill intentions.

I remember one day, his parents had gone out for the day, and they lived next to our unit.

We heard this thunderous banging and noises coming from outside. On further investigation, we found him standing and almost knocking down the door. The Hoo Hoo sounds were ongoing as he was confused because they didn't open the door for him. It took us some time to communicate this with him before my mother explained it in sign language and understood that he would have to return later.

## *Saying Goodbye*

My Granddad had been hospitalized for a few weeks, deteriorating from cancer. My mum had said this was probably his time, but I didn't grasp it as a young person with no-death experience.

One night, we'd gone out partying — it was 4 a.m. when we finally arrived at my friend's house — and I became suddenly overwhelmed by fear, love, and urgency to visit my grandfather in the hospital.

I must have still been intoxicated, yet I pleaded with the hospital staff so they would let me in. Fortunately, they agreed on one condition: I must try and convince my Granddad to take the medicine, which they could not get him to accept.

That night with him, I had a heart-to-heart conversation unlike any before. I could see the fear in his eyes as he reluctantly accepted the medicated yogurt I fed him with a spoon. That's when I realized how alone we can be when the time comes to say our goodbyes. Writing this brings tears to my eyes, but I know he is still watching over me every day of my life.

I stayed with my grandfather until he had calmed down and was ready to drift off to sleep so I could depart for the evening.

The next day, my mother told me that Grandpa had spoken of a visitation from me the night before. They couldn't believe it as they hadn't known I had been there to comfort him.

He passed away shortly after, and this made me realize how connected we are with those beyond our realm, that we can communicate with them in some capacity, or at least they can assist us on our journey through life.

I love you, Morfar & Mormor

∞ ∞ ∞

## Uninvited Houseguest

After leaving my dad's place, I returned to my hometown and stayed between my mom's house and my girlfriend's apartment. One night, as we were in bed, a stranger walked in and got ready to sleep without permission. It was usually just us two since her roommate wasn't there often. So when we heard the front door open one evening, we figured it must be her coming home late from a night out and deciding to sleep over. The entrance was secured with a locking system, so only people with access could enter.

We were taken aback when an unknown man wearing nothing but his boxers showed up in their bedroom.

The girls had a shared bedroom with beds on each side of the room, which worked out fine. When the friend was home, I would stay at my mum's; when she wasn't there, I could stay over.

So, out of the blue, an unfamiliar man appears in the bedroom, then quickly turns around and heads to the kitchen. I turn to my girlfriend with a confused look and ask, "Who was that?" she mimics I don't fucking know!

I listen as he opens the fridge and helps himself to a drink. Not wanting to wait any longer, I confront him as he passes me back to the bedroom. My voice was loud and clear, and I demanded to know what was happening. He doesn't answer me; instead, he brushes past me and into the bedroom, where my girlfriend looks petrified.

He quickly went to the other unoccupied bed and tucked himself in without saying a word. I pulled on his arm, asking him again what was going on. He mumbled some half-asleep response, trying to ignore me by pulling the covers over his head. I flick the lights on and shake him while questioning in disbelief, "What the fuck are you doing?"

He suddenly realized the shift in my voice meant this was not a joke, so he opened his eyes wide and gazed at me in confusion. I told him he wasn't living there and had to go before things got heated. It appeared he finally comprehended the severity of the scenario and muttered an apology before hastily walking out with me close behind him.

As he stepped out of the hallway into the unit across from ours, I watched him shut the door behind him. My girlfriend and I breathed a sigh of relief before locking our door securely.

The next day, I went to knock on his door. He appeared very apologetic and explained that he had gotten so drunk that when trying to go home, he entered our apartment by mistake, which was an exact mirror image of his, only back to front. Although disoriented, he still tried to make it to bed in his drunken state.

## Dodgy Dealings

During the 90s, I was well-versed in the local drug trade and worked part-time for one of the primary dealers in town who had been assigned community service. This arrangement complemented my lifestyle, as I had nothing better to do.

Most customers were booked in advance, so there were few surprises. Drugs were hidden in a pair of rolled-up socks behind a couch cushion to avoid trouble. They could easily be thrown out of the side window and onto a neighbor's property with thick bushes to provide cover. The old house always betrayed visitors' presence before they knocked on the door, as the creaking stairs served as an early warning system.

The air was thick with tension as each individual entered the room, carefully avoiding eye contact while anxiously awaiting their turn.

You never knew how people would react. Security codes were written on slips of paper to protect against any unexpected authorities arriving on the scene, a code known only to those in the know. Though from different walks of life, it was always intriguing when a familiar face appeared—like my old school teacher or the local union councilman. Despite being there to help these people settle their debts, I couldn't help but feel some naughty pleasure in watching their shock and dismay. This place experienced a high turnover rate, and every trick had been used to keep it running smoothly. When a new shipment arrived, usually kilograms of hash, a fresh plate of hash was run across the floors, walls, etc., to infuse the scent on everything inside the apartment. This was done to disorientate police dogs if they showed up, as they wouldn't know which area to focus on, making them obsolete to be used in the searches. The delivery would then be split into selling sizes and taken out to a secret field only the main guy's Wolf Dog knew about. The stash would then be buried underground until more was needed.

# Chapter 11

## Assaulted Awake

### 1998

I abruptly awoke from my slumber, my heart racing to the feeling of something cold and hard pressing against my nose. As my eyes adjusted to the darkness, The M75 standard model assault rifle of the Danish Army shone menacingly in the darkness as I clenched my sphincter and struggled to comprehend what was happening.

Suddenly, two figures stepped out of the shadows with their weapons. It was only then that I recognized them; before I realized what was happening, I saw a bright white smile amidst the shadows before my two friends stepped forward in full body armor and still wearing camouflage fatigues.

Adrenaline coursing through me, we laughed as they told me they had been on patrol with the National Guard. Then they snuck off again, and I watched them fire several rounds into the air in the street before bursting into laughter and disappearing into the night.

## Sorry Granny

My best friend and I had planned a train ride and would smoke a bong on the trip.

This train differed from the train we would typically use with the coupes, so everyone was seated in two seats on either side of the carriage. Only every second window had a small part that could open for air to go in or out.

Then, we also had to keep a lookout to make sure after you had drawn the hit, you had time to stand up, put your mouth close to the open window, and blow the smoke out so no one could smell it.

This worked fine, and we had done this many times before.

This day, though, the conductor arrived just as I was taking a hit. My mate hit my back to alert me, but this also made me cough the entire content out and make it slowly rise from under the seat In front of us, where an elderly lady was sitting!

We quickly put everything away before the conductor came to our seats. He just gave the old lady a weird glance on the way past, and we were out of trouble, just trying not to start laughing and blow our cover. (Pun intended)

Sorry Granny.

## Station Wagon With A Shady Past

We were on a city drive with our buddy, who had bought a cheap station wagon. Sadly, he didn't tell us the local biker gang had used it in shady deals.

We had a fantastic night before we rolled into the town, where the car was well-known by everyone but us.

We noticed one particular car kept showing up, and when we stopped at a set of lights, five big guys were crammed inside it, giving us suspicious looks.

Then, a white van full of patched members pulled up behind us, and we screamed for the driver to run the red light so that we could get away.

It's unbelievable how powerless you feel while sitting helplessly in this metal box when there is no escape plan if things go wrong.

We screamed at the driver and slapped his shoulder to run the red light. And he takes a sharp left up the main street, and we see the van follow us. We can tell the other car has stayed back but cut off the road.

As we go further up, we notice that the road is blocked off due to construction.

We told our driver to pull over and wait until the van got close enough. As we watched them peek into our car from their windows, we got the driver to floor it and do a U-turn so fast the wheels were skidding as the van pulled up right in front of us; they had anticipated our move. We hit the gas, going full speed towards the lights where the other car had blocked the middle of the road. The van trails behind, taking several turns to catch up with us as its turning circle slows down. We race towards the car blocking our path, swerving around them just enough to make it past before hitting the accelerator again and speeding through town. Running several red lights, we create some distance between us and our pursuers.

We had been driving for miles, and the chase was still close behind us until we finally managed to outrun them. Everyone in the car was filled with adrenaline as we cheered the driver on, urging them to go faster than ever before to ensure our escape.

No one spoke until we were about 10 kilometers away and out of sight. Our plans shifted: we were focused on dumping the car and then retreating to our homes where no one would know our whereabouts. We decided to lay low until morning.

## New Year's Eve 1999

We had made it to Freetown Christiania (Danish: *Fristaden Christiania*), also known as Christiania or simply the *Staden*, an intentional community and commune in the Christianshavn neighborhood of the Danish capital city of Copenhagen. It began in 1971 as a squatted military base. Its Pusher Street is famous for its open trade of cannabis, which is illegal in Denmark.

We bought mushrooms to kick the night off, ate them around 11 p.m., settled into a small bar in the Freetown, ordered a few beers, and rolled up a joint to start the evening.

We were enjoying the night until a brawl erupted near our seats. It was no ordinary fight; a person was beaten brutally and covered in blood. We attempted to keep out of it while the psychedelic mushrooms began to take effect. Soon enough, the fight had ended, but now a giant rocket was launched into the bar area though the door, exploding and sending everyone scrambling for cover. A fire started in the wooden frame of the seating area, and two fire extinguishers were needed to put it out before the smoke cleared.

By this time, the mushrooms had definitely started to take effect, and our perception of reality had changed significantly. We decided to go outside and move around a bit to clear our minds.

As the clock struck twelve, rockets were set off by millions of people in the capital. The wooden sticks attached to them were raining down all around us, making our mushroom trip even more chaotic. We quickly ran towards a small roof near the bar to seek cover from the falling sticks and pieces of rockets that sounded like pebbles being thrown around for nearly five minutes. Once the show ended, we moved on in search of a more private place to enjoy the night and our mushroom-induced state.

We were making progress for a few kilometers until we reached the bridge where we were supposed to be going for an after-party. Autonomist Marxists, a left-wing political and social movement against capitalism, had barricaded the bridge. The scene was chaotic as the Autonomists, armed with bricks and fireworks, clashed with hundreds of police officers lined up on one side with riot shields and batons in hand. Our mushroom-induced high increased as we moved past this scene and continued onward.

Due to the bridge being closed, it took us two hours to walk to our destination in Copenhagen. On the way, we encountered a plethora of intoxicated and rowdy people. Soon after, a fight broke out between several men and one who seemed to be fending them off while backing away down the street. We followed them down the road until we reached the flat where we were headed. We dart inside and lock the door behind us since it's on the fifth floor. From our vantage point, we can see that the lone person gets beaten by the gang before they scatter.

We debate if we should run out and help the man, but the effects of our substance use have us all hesitating to go outside. He has woken up from his beating and is now shouting at the group and warning them that he will make them pay. The assailants regroup to finish what they started, but the guy now has new energy. He begins taking down individuals, perhaps because they didn't attack as one unit. Amid this chaotic brouhaha, we called from our doorway for him to come inside so he could hide until the group dispersed and be able to leave undeterred.

The rest of our group had arrived within the hour, and we began the after-party with more beers and bong hits. Our guest was relieved to have a place to hide away while having some fun at the same time. We ended the night enjoying ourselves.

The following day, our bodies ached from the previous night's long walk and chaos. We woke up to the sound of someone knocking on the door. We saw a tall and muscular man standing at the doorstep as we opened it. He introduced himself as the guy in the fight last night and thanked us for having his back.

He explained that he was a local gang member and that they had been hunting him down for a while. He had taken some drugs to numb the pain and stumbled into the fight, not knowing it was a setup. But he had managed to fight back and take down a few of his attackers.

We thanked him for his gratitude and offered him some breakfast. He sat down with us and told us more about his life and struggles living in a gang-infested area.

As he finished his meal, he stood up to leave and reminded us that he would be very grateful for the help and, if we ever needed anything, to reach out.

I recall me and my best friend, Thomas, initial journey to Pusher Street. We copped some top-notch hashish and planned to blaze it up in the middle of the hustle and bustle in a small cafe between the dealers' stands in the middle of Pusher Street. There was just a door with a sign that said 'Cafe.'

We stepped inside the dimly lit bar to find a large, bearded man dressed in a patchwork of psychedelic colors. He waved us over and gestured to a cozy corner booth with an inviting smile. We ordered two bottles of Coke before making our request.

"Can we smoke our bong here?" I asked sheepishly. To this, he shrugged and took a puff from his joint. "Sure, why not? Go ahead and make yourselves comfortable. Let me know if you need anything."

We dumped the pungent hash and tobacco mix into a large glass bong bowl. With one of us holding a lighter in trembling hands, we lit the bong and inhaled deeply. It didn't take long for the effects to hit us—our faces grew hot, and our vision blurred as laughter bubbled inside us. Meanwhile, an Alsatian dog crept around the corner from the café's counter, watching us suspiciously. As paranoia began to set in, it only made us laugh harder.

The door to the room creaked open, and two men stepped in, looking agitated. They were dressed like street-dwellers, sporting sagging jeans and bright colors. One had a gold chain dangling from his neck. We shrunk back against our seats as their voices rose louder than before, and we anxiously waited for them to leave. Their presence was definitely magnified due to our state of being. When they finally did, we got a glimpse of the chaos outside. There was shouting, and people sat on corners peddling their goods while police officers patrolled the area. Our minds raced with paranoia as reality sunk in; we sat in the middle of Pusher Street.

We both erupted in nervous laughter as we slowly shuffled towards the door. After a moment of hesitation, we said our goodbyes and thanks to the café owner. We stepped out into the dusty evening air.

As I glanced around the deserted street, Thomas and I exchanged knowing glances - relieved that our collective paranoia had been unfounded. We sighed a huge breath of relief and had a quick gander with each other about how paranoid the other person was, and then set off for our next adventure, our laughter echoing down the empty street.

# Chapter 12

## The Earth Bong

### 1999

When smoking weed, one of our favorite pastimes was to make an Earth Bong.

This consisted of finding a soft area of dirt and then, with your fingers, digging two holes that meet in the middle, making sure they were firm and compact.

Then, get a handful of small pebbles and fill one hole about two-thirds of the way.

On the other side, you would get the top from a soft drink bottle and cut it off so it would make a small mouthpiece that would fit over the second hole. Then, fill the opposite side with the pebbles and the mixture of weed and roasted tobacco to burn it, and then smoke like this.

The high from this would be utterly different from what you are used to as the dirt and small pebbles would filter the smoke very differently to any pipe or bong and usually outside in nature. The trick was always to build this contraption on a hill. Hence, you had to lie facing downward before inhaling the smoke, which added to the experience.

This could also be achieved inside if you had a large bucket with dirt and built the same way, which we found handy during the winter months when the ground was frozen, and it was too cold outside.

I remember one particular day when we discovered a lovely place behind the house I was living in with my roommates.

There was a large garden that was peaceful and quiet, and it had to be summer for the weather to have been so pleasant. We all wore shorts and t-shirts, lounging around and talking about our day-to-day lives as we made an earth bong.

We had finally prepared it and took turns smoking the large amounts we needed. We settled back as soon as we were done, and the conversations and merriment began.

We continued talking and laughing until someone asked what the time was. At that moment, my friend pointed out that two sizeable orange garden snails close to us were now a couple of meters away. It dawned on us that we'd been sitting in the garden for almost four hours, and night had started falling.

At the thought of a Garden snail's lifestyle—four hours to move two meters—we erupted in laughter, astounded at how long the creature needed to traverse such a short distance.

## *Turning point*

The only time I got kicked out for being a local dealer was weird and embarrassing.

I would get weed for these two brothers; one was older than me, in his late twenties, Big beard, and still lived at his mum's house, and his brother, who was maybe 18 at the time.

I arrived in the afternoon, and they got a few grams of Hashies. We were smoking it when the mum came home, which generally wasn't a problem, but today, she came straight into the room and pointed me out, saying she didn't want me there and I had to leave!

I was more shocked than anything and told her that I had been invited inside. I would leave in a minute, and it was a tense standoff between me smoking one last Bong head and walking out through the living room where she was sitting, waiting to give me a mouthful on the way out. A few remarks flew the other way.

## A Turkish Connection And A look Into The Underworld

I knew I needed to try and get a new start again and get away from the small town where we were, as there was no future for me to get ahead in life.

So, I enrolled in a sports college, studying shooting, outdoor life, and multiple other sports. One of my friends there was a Turkish man, just like me, a bit older than the average student. We ended up in the same massage course together. We were the only two without partners, so we had to pair up and give each other our massage for our certificates. Even though it was awkward, we got through it and eventually finished with a face massage, where we fell asleep.

We started talking often after that. We would hang out together outside of school since we all lived in two-bedroom units connected to the college. We'd chat, drink beers, and party with the other students. During these times, he told me about his network from the city of Aarhus near our school, how he used to be one of the biggest cocaine dealers in town, and that this helped us get into various places—like nightclubs—without any trouble.

One day, he asked me to accompany him to a gaming area with several slot machines; he and his connections rented them out for profit. They hadn't been paid their rent in some time, so we arrived expecting the people who owned up the money to have sorted itself out by now—he said all I needed to do was stand near the door, which was enough to make them pay up.

So, on arrival, my friend started the discussion to get what was owed, and they kept talking in circles. It was getting nowhere, but at some point, they realized he wasn't budging, so my friend looked at me a few times, and I looked at them occasionally to make it clear that the debt was due today.

After much loud debating, they decided to check an old pokie machine with enough stacks of money tucked away inside the back to cover the amount owed. Once that was settled, we celebrated with some drinks and continued our day like nothing had happened.

On another occasion, we had a quiet night and were both bored, so he told me to hop in the car, and he would show me something.

We arrived at a deserted shopping mall around 10 p.m., and I asked what we were doing, only to be told to wait and see. We exited the van and descended the stairs to a large metal door below the center. My Turkish brother went first, and a tiny camera in one corner monitored the entrance. He pressed a buzzer, and someone inside inquired who it was. After he answered, a buzzer sounded, and the door swung open.

The first room we entered had a humongous 50-inch T.V. with two sofas surrounding it and many people smoking marijuana while watching movies. They all waved hello as we passed by – everyone seemed content. Then, we moved into an empty room with fluorescent symbols all over the walls that glowed under U.V. lighting. As the music got louder, we stepped onto a dance floor with a bar at one corner and arcade machines in another, plus a smaller dance floor space similar to the one without anyone in it – walls decorated with neon symbols lit up by U.V. illumination. The bartender knew who had arrived and asked how he was doing before offering us drinks. A few girls were dancing to techno in the packed little room, probably having taken something before; their bodies swayed gracefully in tune with the beat. In front of the arcade machine stood a Hells Angel biker dressed in his leather cut, playing games while sipping his beer in peace.

After a couple of drinks and lively conversation, we explored the rest of town. This secret hangout for the local underworld was quite a surprise - I had no idea it was right under my feet.

On our way back to college, my friend spotted a car he thought he recognized and pulled into a dark car park. He honked the horn several times, and a man in all black with his face half concealed by a balaclava appeared from the shadows with a grin when he saw who it was. He shouted out, 'Thank goodness it's you!' We had assumed he was an undercover cop as we would do some unspoken tasks that night. My friend jokingly scolded them for wasting their time on such illicit activities, and we drove off, still chuckling about the events of the evening.

This was not the perfect change, but I quit smoking dope daily, my fitness returned, and I was moving towards a better outcome and future.

The longer I stayed, the more I could gather myself to get away from being stuck in the small town I came from and find a purpose in life and a goal to work towards.

Later, We went skiing with our sports school in Norway and brought our Alcohol since it was five times more expensive there. Of course, we had some hard liquor that, combined with the chilly weather, created a chaotic situation.

We were all at the nightclub near the ski resort, and my friend was being harassed on the dance floor by some locals trying to start a fight. I jumped in and started dancing, pretending to be part of the fun. One of them puts a shoulder tackle on me. I ignored this and kept moving around like I didn't notice. Still, I saw out of the corner of my eye that he had sent a kick toward my head, so I quickly ducked under his foot, delivered a dirty overhand punch to his face, and laid him out cold.

Immediately, bouncers and some locals crowded around me, forcing me to move backward into the corner and leaving me to wait for the next move. Before any of them could throw a punch, the bouncers had hurriedly taken me out of the bar while keeping my friends inside since they seemed to know each other already.

I stood alone in the snow, surrounded by four local thugs. I was drunk and angry enough to take on all of them at once. They slowly began to close in, tightening their circle as my heart raced with panic. One spoke in broken English with a menacing smirk, warning me that I was going down hard. With a surge of adrenaline, I braced myself for the first attack and prepared to fight like a madman until help arrived.

I was drunk enough to know running wouldn't help me, but I was clear-headed enough to know I could fight, so I decided to fight back. I stared him straight in the eyes and challenged him, "I like big trouble." He made no move - my readiness for a brawl was evident in my expression. I had my fists clenched and at the ready. If either of them had made a single move, I would have attacked like an injured animal. This gave my friends enough time to get past the bouncers, who had blocked them inside and then ran to assist me with the fight. By this point, these fellows didn't want any part of it and quickly scampered away, even as they called out some insults on their way.

During my time here, I resurrected my passion for sewing again and was the only guy with 20 girls during a sewing course for 2 hours twice per week. Not a bad deal and I enjoyed this time surrounded by girls who always asked for help. I made several new clothes and learned so much more from the teacher, who was eager to teach me more advanced techniques and ended up sewing my suit jacket and other more advanced items.

The girls, in general, weren't too pleased with me being there as they would struggle to make simple designs, such as a wallet, and I would walk out with two pairs of pants and a shirt after a 2 hours session.

But they still found it extraordinary that I would do this without feeling hesitant just because it wasn't a boy thing to do.

It was at the sports college that one day, they had a seminar on a guy who had borrowed his dad's sailboat and was going to sail to the U.K. and back, which was planned for a 2-week trip.

But as he arrived at his destination in England, met some more people traveling, and talked to them about sailing his boat to the Caribbean with them, he changed his plans. Then he called his dad and asked if it was okay for him to do this, and he wasn't sure when he would be back.' The dad encouraged the trip, and off he went.

He didn't return home for over two years. He traveled around the world in a sailboat. He met some fantastic people while sometimes staying on almost deserted islands and other times in large cities and making lifelong friends before leaving for the next port several months later.

This really struck a chord with me, and I could shake this idea out of my mind, so a month or so before the sports school finished, I had arranged tickets to fly to the U.K. and contact a lady who could get me live-in jobs as soon as I was there.

This was my way out: take a risk, leave the small-time town behind, and make a future for myself.

I had planned to return home for a week before leaving, see everyone I wanted to say goodbye to, and then off on my adventure.

The week home was a blur as I went from party to party to see as many people as possible, and it went much quicker than I could have imagined.

I did, however, catch up with the girl I had missed out on some years earlier, and every time we met, we were with someone else. But this time, nothing stood between us from having the best time together and making the most of it. However, she was seeing someone at the time; it came second to what we had, and this time was for us to rekindle that even though our time was on the clock again. We had to move in different directions within the week ending again.

Sunday morning, I had stayed up all night to say my goodbyes. I went home in the early morning to say goodbye to my mum. She drove me to the airport in Copenhagen, and my new life was about to start. It was hard, and I wanted to stay with the girl I wanted and do small-town life again. Still, I knew deep down I needed to keep moving forward and not let that small town destroy me. I could come back later when I conquered my inner demons and became a mentally strong man who knew what life had to bring and how to help others in need.

As the plane took off, I cried, thinking of the life I had left behind. Still, I was excited about the prospect of what I could achieve and the adventures just around the corner.

Only 1-hour flight and I landed at Heathrow airport in the U.K. I took a train towards my first destination, the small campsite where I could for a few days until I secured a job which had been preplanned and arranged.

# Chapter 13

## The United Kingdom

### 2000

Stepping onto U.K. soil, after hours of searching, I was sadly informed that my campsite had vanished. After aimlessly wandering with my backpack for hours in a low-income area, with many eyes watching me, the lost white boy, I even spotted a homeless man huddling by a fire barrel—something I'd only ever seen in movies. So I decided to splurge on the only hotel around, an upscale four-star hotel for the night, and reach out to the woman running the website offering live-in job opportunities nationwide.

Eventually, I got a spot to stay and work at a pub in the countryside outside of Reading. I landed in England at the start of the 2000s with one phone number belonging to the lady behind said website. Once I had arrived, all it took was one call, and she would start finding me a place to stay. Our connection point was meeting beneath an Australian flag outside of Reading Station in the heart of England.

I met the landlord at Reading station, and my first stop in England was a pub called the King William, not exactly the most bustling of places. I got a job as a dishwasher and kitchen porter, where I was offered a caravan behind the pub to live in and earned 140 pounds per week in addition to free meals.

There was an amazing little zoo not far away from this place, though it consisted of a small entry fee, and you could then buy bags of food for the animals.

The animals were a small selection of birds, goats, cows, some meerkats, a couple of emus, and pigs while all over the place there would be Guinea pigs running around like some small herds counting maybe 5 to 10 pigs and in total, possibly 100, which I found pretty amusing because they were constantly squeaking and look funny in general.

My little brother had come to visit for a few days. I managed to get a picture of one of the emus biting his hand as I set him up, telling him that although they looked scary, they would take the seeds from his hand as gently as a fly landing, where the reality was very different and created a fantastic picture taken with a single use camera which at today's standards but be unknown and then the realization as to the timing of getting the image is 1 in a million.

It lasted about two months until the head chef I had been getting on with offered to arrange another job at a better place with better pay.

He could see I needed to find a place where there were some young people around and places to go.

I said my goodbyes and was happy to see the back of the trailer I had called home for the beginning of this trip.

∞ ∞ ∞

## A Wild Sunday Afternoon At The Pub

This evening still stands clear as day in my head.

My curiosity was piqued as I arrived at the Bull and Butcher, a bustling and upscale English pub/restaurant in Turville, England's quaint village. The Sunday afternoon sun cast a warm glow on the scene before me. It seemed like the perfect place to escape the confines of my current living situation - a weird caravan prison. Having previously explored this charming establishment, thanks to the chef's generous invitation, I looked forward to reconnecting with familiar faces and indulging in camaraderie. The locals I had befriended during my previous visits were always up for a good time, sharing laughs over pints of beer. That evening, as I stepped through the door of the Bull and Butcher, I was immediately enveloped in an atmosphere of friendliness and joy. The clinking of glasses and the hum of animated conversations filled the air. It was as if the world outside ceased to exist, and only this lively sanctuary remained. I joined a group of like-minded individuals eager to escape my caravan-induced isolation. As the hours passed, I reveled in the joy of newfound friendship and the simple pleasure of human connection. I lived in a caravan with little communication with the outside world. Most of the entertainment came from playing on a PlayStation 1 and masturbating because, after 9 p.m., the place was a ghost town; that's not even right; it was a ghost pub with nothing around, not even street lights, only the regular bang coming from the scarecrow electronic gunshot machine which was installed on the farm further down the road to keep the fields free from birds.

The only times I would get out was when the chef would take me out. I connected with one of the bar girls, and she would take me out. Still, it felt like she was doing it because she felt sorry more than being interested in me, so it always felt awkward and died off quickly after I left.

The bar was filled with a few regular patrons, one of whom was a sheep farmer and his apprentice. Then there was the boisterous one who always wanted to be the center of attention and was usually the one to have some nose beers *Cocaine* that kept everyone's spirits high throughout the night.

This person, "let's call him Steve," had obviously arranged with the sheep farmer to challenge the apprentice in a game for ten quid per game.

The game rules were mesmerizing as Steve was experienced in entertaining a crowd and proceeded to pull out some condoms, which he had gotten from the public toilets in the pub while engaging in his other habit.

He would open one up and, with both his hands, pull it over his head, covering the eyes and nose, and then holding tight as he would inhale through the mouth and then exhale out his nose to start blowing up the condom on his head, representing some weird cone head alien shape, which was very amusing to watch and how this game would progress.

The barter would start, and the farmer would put down one crisp ten quid bill on the table. He would say that he could blow up a condom faster than the apprentice until it would explode, which would determine the game's winner.

Having had several pints of beer and keen to show off for the local crowd, the apprentice was quick to slam down his ten quid, and the game would begin.

Of course, the instigator, "Steve," would control the game and always put the condom on the apprentice first and then follow the sheep farmer. However, while doing the condom on the farmer, he would rip the condom, so he had already won. Still, the apprentice had no idea because the condom covered his eyes, so he couldn't see this.

The apprentice, with the condom now strapped over his eyes and nose, was being attended to by the crowd that formed around the two due to its obvious entertainment value. Steve puts a condom on the farmer's head. The crowd cheers, and Steve begins the count for them to start inflating the condoms; before long, everyone leans in to see if the condom will burst.

At the start of each game, the apprentice would blow as hard as he could, sometimes nearly blacking out. As a result, the condom was sent soaring toward the ceiling and stayed at least three feet above his head. The onlookers would cheer him on as they watched the climax that never came. Eventually, Steve would step up and pop his balloon with a needle since his breath wasn't enough to burst it. Despite this, he felt he was just a moment away from winning due to the spectators' encouraging chants.

This was an unforgettable experience, and the apprentice was none the wiser when they left at the end of the night; he owed the farmer 40 quid, and he was blind drunk after all the beers and the heavy exhaling into the condoms.

I began my job washing dishes and helping out in the kitchen. By observing the chefs, I picked up some cooking skills and eventually started assisting them with meals. After a year, I had advanced up the ranks due to others leaving and my increasing skill level. Over this time, I worked with three head chefs and a few who were filling in for holidays or any change of head chef. This allowed me to learn from them all, making me the go-to person for checking on popular meals, staffing during busier hours, etc. On occasion, I even filled in as head chef at the pub.

The pub had a Bib Armand, listed in the Michelin Guide as an award-winning service and food location. This recognition brought more customers to the restaurant and made it widely known.

One morning, the Bar manager rushed in to tell us that a food critic was coming for lunch and would rate our pub. I was in charge of the kitchen then, so my job was to watch out for the critic's order and ensure it was cooked to perfection if possible. Fortunately, we could pull off serving the critic without much trouble. He seemed satisfied with his grilled salmon steak and vegetables but commented about the service time and décor. Everyone breathed a collective sigh of relief.

The village was renowned for being featured in various TV programs and films. It boasted a stunning landscape with the iconic windmill from the movie Chitty Chitty Bang Bang perched atop the eastern hills. At the heart of the village was the church, which had made appearances in The Vicar of Dibley and Midsummer Murders — two hugely popular TV shows at one point.

## Downward Spiral of Posh Landlords

The pub was owned by a middle-aged Landlord and Lady who appeared to thrive on the successes of yesteryear. However, it was all too apparent that their attempts at poshness needed to be improved as they struggled to keep up with the ongoing changes in the industry. The business was moving downwards, and they had already sold off their expensive vehicles to stay afloat. It seemed inevitable that they would lose the pub, their claim to fame.

I vividly recall one particular evening when the bar manager vocalized his disapproval of how the pub was being run. He mentioned that the landlords would often show up with a wireless baby monitor. This technological gadget allowed them to monitor their child from afar. The two-way radio sender could be plugged into an outlet near the infant and connected to another socket in a different part of the house. Every time the child made a noise or moved, the parents received sound alerts, and a collared display would glow in different colors and brightness based on how much noise was emitted.

To my surprise, whenever the Landlord and Lady visited the pub, they would bring along this device and plug it in at the end of the bar - right in plain view of everyone. Mind you, they didn't live in the pub but resided 3-4 houses away around a corner. I'm still unsure how effective this gadget was, but it worked for them. Most times, you'd see its lights glowing and hear some sound alerts, indicating that the child was making sounds or moving around.

But just as often, the same hollow answer of "It's just static or interference" would come. They'd turn down the sound and return to their usual activities: drinking, boasting of their successes, and craving the attention that made them feel like kings.

This particular evening was the same, with only a handful of locals present. The bar manager had been vocal about what he deemed unacceptable in this establishment.

Then suddenly, the landlady arrived, striding confidently

toward the bar and sitting down with an air of importance, wearing her usual gold necklaces and expensive jewelry, demanding a large glass of Pinot Grigio white wine. The bar manager replied sweetly that he could oblige - but asked her to wait a moment while he went to fetch it from the other side of the bar. His smile was anything but warm.

The landlady is, as usual, making sure everyone has noticed her and that she is the center of attention.

Only a few minutes later, the bar manager returns with the large glass of Pinot, serves it to the landlady with a big bright smile, and tells her to enjoy this delicate grape.

The bar manager walks straight to our table, places his hands on it, then leans close to us. His eyes first glance at the landlady before turning back to us. He glares, and his beard crinkles as he breathes slowly, like a cartoon character about to blow up at someone. The other guests divert their eyes or stare into their drinks so they don't catch the manager's eye but hang on to his words. The smoke goes dead in the room. "I hope," he says after a pause, leaning in further, that she enjoys the wine because he had stirred it with his Cock in the other bar before serving it and then laughed and walked back to the bar.

After a few minutes, two individuals with clipboards and an air of authority came into the pub looking for the proprietors. They wanted to know where their child was at that exact moment. The atmosphere in the room became instantly uncomfortable as it dawned on those present what was happening. Nobody watched what unfolded, but the rumors about the mysterious occurrences at the pub didn't stop after that night. The child was not taken away, although they got a severe warning from child services, and things did change. Still, the static/interference story was not unheard of even after that night.

## *Sad Richness*

Most weekends, a small, rotund rich man would stroll into the local pub with an air of arrogance. He drove a red Ferrari convertible and never missed an opportunity to boast about it.

The conversation always centered around him and his success and whatever car he was driving that day to show off. His usual trick was to drive his red Ferrari through the small town and gun the engine to make the exhaust pipe sound like a war drum in the valley. Then, after ensuring everyone noticed him, he'd speed away in the opposite direction. Within fifteen minutes, he'd be back, having changed into his yellow Ferrari, and do it all over again. Finally, he'd roll up in his Range Rover and park it outside the pub while he flaunted his wealth inside.

Whenever someone asked why he bought the Yellow Ferrari, since it was the same model as the red one, he'd get a kick out of responding with "Because I had the red one." His little stained pig's teeth would always peek out from his mouth when he laughed, and those moments filled him with joy.

The landlord at the time was pretty eccentric. He had no problem coming up with new and slightly questionable ideas to get customers in the doors.

One such idea had arrived early in the morning before we got in the kitchen. As we arrived, a couple of large black plastic bags were sitting on the kitchen counter.

Upon opening them, we found 36 freshly killed grey squirrels, which was a bit of a shock as in, can we even cook them? And is it legal?

After asking around, it was confirmed that they are a pest in the UK and, as such, could be killed on sight. My main problem was the ethics of this rodent being prepared as a meal for paying customers.

I advised them I didn't want anything to do with this. Still, the relief chef at the time didn't care as he got paid very good money to help, and then a local crocodile Dundee, was in the bar when the discussion happened.

He was dressed in cowboy boots, jeans, a flannel jacket with a leather vest on top, and already had a large knife on his hip; he stated that he had never skinned a squirrel, so he was happy to help for the experience.

It took the three people 3 hours to skin the 36 squirrels. It produced very little meat but enough for about eight pies and a Squirrel stew, which the landlord then triumphantly put on the specials board for the next week's specials.

I tasted it, and it wasn't too bad; it tasted like a cross between Deer and chicken meat.

For all the time I was there, one of our best sellers was the Cajun Chicken salad, which would easily sell 60 portions per week and was always in high demand.


On the top of the valley was John Paul Getty's estate, and at the time, he was known as the wealthiest man in the UK.

The estate had 22 houses and a pub, which was run specifically for the staff, who all got a home and a car with the job.

The Gardner had a Ferrari lawnmower, estimated to cost 120,000 pounds, and was a large red, fully electronic monstrosity with a yellow Ferrari logo on the side.

Many of his staff were locals at the bull and butcher, and we heard many stories of life on his estate.

One was about a chef who had just been employed and had got a Subaru Impreza rally model as his company car and, two weeks into the job, wrapped it around a tree, driving home from the pub drunk.

He left the car, walked home, and fell asleep, to be woken by the secretary on the phone telling him they knew what had happened and not to discuss it with anyone.

Then, he went out and checked his mail, and there were keys for a brand new Subaru, which had been parked in his driveway, ready to go to work.

Yearly, Getty would also have some of the biggest cricket teams attend his private course on his estate. After wintering in the UK, it would always have a large brown patch on the north end of the pitch, which, from word of mouth, he would have replaced every year for 150,000 pounds so it looked nice.

Another story was that the cricket world had three very expensive trucks which would be used to suck the water out of the pitches before games. Getty owned 2 of these three trucks but was always sending them around the world to any cricket pitch that needed it free of charge.

And, of course, the most famous story was that of his son being kidnapped in 1973. the prominent Italian Mafia abducted John Paul Getty III in Rome and requested 17 million dollars (112 million dollars in current terms) for his return. The family believed it to be a ploy by their rebellious son to get money from his tightfisted grandfather. J. Paul Getty denied John Paul's request, pointing out that paying would also make his other 13 grandchildren targets for kidnapping. After three weeks of waiting due to an Italian postal strike, a newspaper received an envelope with some hair and what appeared to be a human ear. They were informed if they did not pay 3.2 million dollars for Paul's safe return, he would be "sent back in little bits."

The kidnappers eventually agreed to a ransom of $3 million. J. Paul Getty, however, only wanted to pay the maximum amount that would be tax-deductible, which was $2.2 million (an equivalent of $14.5 million in 2022). He loaned his grandson the remaining $800,000 with an interest rate of four percent. On December 15, 1973, Getty's grandson was found alive near a Lauria fuel station in the Potenza province, just after the money had been sent.

∞ ∞ ∞

*Turville Heath*

When I shared a cottage on the heath with my fiancé, I relished the mornings I rode my bike to work. All around me were stunning views and feelings of invigoration from the morning air and dew. One day, as I rounded the corner and started down a two-kilometer stretch of road between large fields, I was taken aback by what I saw.

As far as the eye could see, there must have been more than one thousand pheasants covering every field and the road. I took a moment to determine how best to push through them and decided to pedal fast and make some noise. So, with a hard kick of my feet against the pedals, I picked up speed before the chaos began. The birds moved away from me, but their automatic responses were erratic, much like when a rabbit saw a car's headlights.

For the next few minutes, I was dealing with a barrage of birds all around me as I tried to keep my handlebars straight and make it to the end without crashing. I eventually made it but promised myself I would return for my car next time.

One particular morning, I decided to take a different route that passed Lord Sainsbury's estate. It was common knowledge that you could enter the estate via its paddocks and bridleways, provided you closed them after passing through.

As I rode towards the estate's gatehouse, I noticed a man I hadn't seen before leap out from nowhere with his hand up, demanding me to stop. Startled by this unexpected request, I quickly swerved around him and kept biking down the road. The man shouted something at me again and started chasing after me on foot, but he had no chance of catching up to me because I was on my mountain bike. However, when I reached the gate 100 meters further down, I had to stop and open it to continue on my path. Turning back, I saw this guy still running after me as if he wanted to murder me. I pushed my bike inside the gate and locked it in a hurry before he got too close. Then, with a wave goodbye in his direction, I sped away down the hill en route to work.

The local people loved hearing about my adventure with the wealthy people's staff member in the pub that morning.

∞ ∞ ∞

## The Fallen Tree & The Pompous Lawyer

In a pivotal moment of my life, I had achieved something extraordinary.

My time at the Bull and Butcher, working my way from being the kitchen porter to the second chef, was full of unforgettable moments, none more so than when I met the head Gardner at Mrs. Ford's Estate. We instantly felt a strong connection between us, and it wasn't long before we were living together in a cozy flint cottage steps away from Mrs. Ford's Estate.

I was working as an under Gardner and dating the head Gardner! We were deeply in love, and she had arranged for me to become a Gardner and live together in a flint cottage only five minutes from the estate. The entire experience was provided by her job as the Head-Gardner.

This relationship shook my world. We shared something deeply passionate that could not be denied. However, after a few years, our flame ultimately faded away. Yet, I never regret what we felt together during those days and nights.

On one particular day, although I had heard rumors about Mrs. Ford being a little particular about real life and how we commoners were operating, this story takes the cake.

One story stands out where the Gardner's had to arrange for one apple tree, be made to grow in the same direction and several others by using ropes to make it look the same!

But in this particular incident, there had been a huge storm. One of the trees in the forest at the back of the estate had fallen and had left an enormous hole. The tree, which would have been maybe 3 meters wide at least and about 60 meters tall, crashed down and blocked the path in this area.

The forest may have been small, but it was meticulously maintained. It took weeks and multiple workers to mow the grass within it using a ride-on lawnmower and then haul away the clippings. This task had been completed just days before Mrs. Ford's annual visitation of her estate, so this presented an issue for everyone concerned; whatever action was taken would most certainly come under her scrutiny. So, it was decided that waiting was the best course of action to ensure that the job could be done to Mrs. Ford's satisfaction.

Honey fungi had crawled through the tree's limbs and into its roots, choking off life and causing rot. The morning they arrived, everyone was walking to the area in question, including the two estate managers, the chauffer, the head Gartner two under Gartner's, and Mrs. Ford and her boyfriend, whom the story was was one of the highest paid lawyers in the world. The scent of sap and freshly cut grass wafted in the morning breeze. As we approached the area, birds could be heard singing. We were met with a large tree estimated to be at least 100 years old, in its prime, standing at a towering height of over 60 meters and nearly three meters across. A colossal crater existed at its base, easily deep and wide enough to fit an automobile.

Amidst the heated debate among the leadership, the famous lawyer suddenly stepped in and proclaimed, "Let's do what we did at our Palm Beach, Florida estate. We dug a hole, put the tree back in it, and it re-rooted!"

At that moment, I looked around and felt the urge to laugh. But the estate manager's eyes flashed like lightning when I did, reminding me that this pompous, upper-crust lawyer had no idea of the real world. He may have been in charge, but I knew I couldn't let him catch me laughing, so I forced it down and quickly retreated before he could hear me.

## Cigarette Breaks Can Be Deadly

I was employed as a Gardner at Mrs. Ford's Estate.

One morning during our fifteen-minute break, I rushed out to buy cigarettes at the local pub in an old light blue Peugeot GT station wagon.

Driving on English rural roads can be quite challenging. The roads are usually narrow and barely fit two cars at a time; substantial side hedges block your view. For these reasons, I preferred driving at night to get a warning from car headlights before colliding with another vehicle.

You never knew what kind of surprise awaited you around the corner. Some rich kid teen in their Ferrari or a considerable truck might come flying by. Most of those encounters ended with both vehicles slamming on the brakes and pulling into the hedge on the left side. We'd then nod apologetically and wave to one another before reversing back onto a passing area so we could pass each other safely.

On this particular day, it was lightly raining, and I had to hurry because I only had fifteen minutes left for my break.

As I approached the Y junction, my heart started racing. The road was straight and empty, but out of nowhere, a gigantic combine harvester appeared before me. It had a huge, round, spinning front end with ten-inch spikes scattered over it like something out of a cartoon nightmare. Panic set in as I realized I was too close to stop in time and going too fast. I pulled the car as far right as possible without hitting the trees. Still, only two wheels remained on the road, while the others were mired in mud and grass that had become slippery due to the rain.

I watched in horror as the rotating spikes from the harvester passed by my window on one side while trees flew past on the other. I knew that even if I made it through this alive, I still wouldn't be able to make the turn ahead since my car was still sliding uncontrollably towards it. My knuckles turned white as I gripped the steering wheel tightly and braced myself for impact before being shot into an unknown void.

Launching off a grassy ledge, the Station wagon flew maybe a meter in the air and then abruptly stopped after skidding down the street.

I just sat there for a few seconds, checking myself and looking around, asking if I had survived.

Incredibly, the car had no visible damage; nothing was wrong with me either; I just had to keep going.

One minute later, another car hurtled around another blind corner. We both hit our brakes hard and ended up bumper-to-bumper. We waved in apology, and the other driver reversed fifty meters back so that we could pass them.

After that, I drove a few minutes to work late but unscathed after two near-death experiences in five minutes — all for some cigarettes, which I didn't even get!

## New Year's Eve drug problems

For the New Year's Eve party in 2001, I went with my Fiancé and her two brothers and partners to a Ministry of the Sound party in an old warehouse in London.

It was a massive complex with DJs playing in separate rooms, and you could roam about and find what type of music you were looking for.

The toilet block was in the middle of them all and consisted of an imperial staircase leading up to them.

This wasn't a big problem, except we had acquired an eight ball of Cocaine and were going to share this once we got to the toilets, the problem being the lineup was all the way down to the bottom, and it never seemed to move. As we stood there waiting and planning what to do to get the night kick-started, I grew impatient and walked past all the people, getting several dirty looks, and made it to the toilets to find there was tons of room; the problem was that there were only about five lockable cubicles and everyone was going in there a few people together at a time. Everyone had the same idea, but no one had the guts to get it done.

So I walked back down, grabbed my group, and told them to follow me up; they were questioning this but reluctantly went up. I showed the empty room, and we could line up the Cocaine on the table next to the sinks. And if we just stood around, we could block from anyone seeing, and there was no one in the room except the people in the cubicles doing drugs anyway.

So we got the drugs lined up and snorted before retreating to the dance floor and getting into the festivities.

This worked great, and we would do the same drill each time we needed another bump for the night.

# Chapter 14

## Florida

### 2001

My fiancé had planned a trip with her younger siblings, and I was invited to join them for a 3-week trip to Florida.

As their flights had been booked a while before I came into the picture, I had to make my own way to Florida airport as the flight they had booked was already full.

The flights went unaspiring, except for the Customs officer when I landed asking how much money I had, where I was staying, etc. I didn't have many answers, except I was meeting my fiancé outside as she was picking me up and then going to our hotel, which she had the name of. After a bit of questioning, he must have seen that I wasn't lying but didn't have the answer I should have; he let me through and just reminded me of the punishment for overstaying a visa before saying have a lovely holiday.

I met my Fiancé outside with her brother and sister, who were excited to get this journey on the way.

The first few nights we spent in a luxurious rental house in the middle of Orlando, with all the trimmings, including a nice pool and air-conditioning, which was more than needed on these 33-degree days.

We all fell straight into holiday mode, played in the pool, and just laid back with a cold drink whenever we felt like it.

The next few days were spent enjoying being away, looking for places to go and have dinners, and planning our trip to visit

Disneyland.

After several attempts to buy tickets and being pressured into attending these timeshare apartment meetings, we ended up in some random place that offered tickets for Universal Studio and Island of Adventure for a reasonable price, with no questions.

We went to the office, and of course, they started the timeshare spiel; I cut them off and said we just wanted the tickets and would not buy any timeshare, no matter how hard they tried.

We agreed on a super quick rundown on their part. Then we could get the tickets for a week of free entry to both parks, which was what we wanted. Thirty minutes later, we walked out with our freedom back. The kids were excited as they had been going through the brochures of these parks, and it would be a fun time. We spent the next week roaming the parks and tried all the big rollercoaster's and rides we could find.

It was nice to have the whole week just to come and go and not have to rush and stand in queues all day but enjoy the place and have a look around, go for a drive and do some shopping before heading home and then arrange dinner being it at home or in a restaurant for that night.

We did have one night out with some friend who was visiting Orlando at the same time at a Pirates theme night, where you get seated around a huge stage and a pirate ship is in the middle. Your pirate, whatever color area you were placed in, would come and introduce himself and talk himself up according to the role he had been given, and then the show would start with the pirates going through their roles as the show moved on until, in the end, there was a winner and during this dinner and drinks were served. In several competitions, the pirates would lose and walk the plank until the winner was crowned and the show was finished.

After that first week, we rented a Wrangler Jeep. We started our journey by driving around Florida to see as much as possible and staying in motels around the coast as we went.

None ever picked up on the map I was using that I had gotten from a McDonald's restaurant, and they found it strange that we always seemed to land for our stopovers near such places.

The days went by, and we saw some fantastic places. One night, someone knocked on the door very late, and I went to check the peephole to see a questionable-looking person outside, asking if this was where the party was. I told him there was no party here, but he was persistent and asked if I could open the door to see if I was telling the truth. I felt this was not right, and I could see him glancing down the hallway as if someone else was waiting.

So I just told him sorry, mate, no party here and then stopped answering his queries. He finally left, and we could get back to sleep after staying alert to see if he returned.

This happened again a few days later at another motel, and it seemed to be the main trick the night people would use to get you to open the door, and then they would storm in and rob you or worse.

So lucky our instinct was right, and we never opened the door or fell for their tactics.

We went around the coast and were halfway down the keys to Key West when we heard a storm was on the way. We were still about a day's drive away, so we turned back and went through Miami to look around. I was a little lost at one point and stopped at a general store for some supplies, not realizing this was probably not the neighborhood for a new jeep full of white people to stop.

As we walked through the car park, I noticed a group of gangsters hanging around in their blue colors, and as we approached, they gave away a look like what the hell was going on.

As we entered the shop, I told the younger brother and sister not to dick around, go in, get what we needed, and then leave again.

They were in holiday mode, so they were playing silly games all the time, making fun of everything they saw, but I managed to get it through to them that this was not fun.

We walk into the shop, and two cash registers are open with Mexican staff members serving only black people; they all stop and stare at us as we walk in.

By now, I realize how bad the situation is, grab hold of them again and tell them to follow us closely. My fiancé could see what was happening, so she stayed beside them. We just grabbed the food and drinks we needed and then went straight for the counter, where the staff had stopped serving the locals, who just stepped aside when we came up and let us get served without question, and the tension was high. Still, it was like they knew we didn't know where we were, and the sooner we were gone, the sooner everyone could relax again.

So we paid, politely thanked them, and went straight for the car, where we could see the group and gang members outside had moved to another side of the shops and were watching our every move.

We rushed to the car as two of them headed our way. We got everyone in and sped away, sweat dripping from our faces. We drove quickly but cautiously, searching for a safe place to stop for the night. We wanted to get off the road and hide away until morning.

## The Business Deal

My job as a gardener had made me acquainted with a computer programmer from South Africa. He was do to marry an English woman employed in one of the area's pubs I frequented and where my fiancée worked on the nights she wasn't home.

We'd spend many nights with our partners or just the boys, going out to watch football at the local pub. We would get some much-needed guy time as we sipped our pints and chatted football and whatever our drunken minds would be bringing up. On a whim, we came up with an entrepreneurial venture: to craft and market websites for small businesses - pubs especially - since we both understood the workings of the industry. Most needed more money or expertise to make their own website. We acted on our vision, buying a decent digital camera and laptop before he coded a program that could create a full-fledged website in under five minutes.

My task was to visit the Pubs, take twelve photos in a predetermined sequence, and then upload them into the program. Afterward, it would generate a website customers could see right away. It was cutting-edge technology for its time, but most thought it was too good to be true, so they decided not to continue with our offer.

My father had a connection to a large firm in Denmark that needed a database constructed for its customers, and I reached an agreement with them. We secured half the money initially, and the other half would be provided once the project was completed. This turned out to be the golden opportunity we were searching for.

This was all fine for a month or so until the client started changing the requirements for the program. My friend worked on the code and asked me to adjust how the software searched for data. There were slight changes here and there, but it was within the parameters of what we had discussed. Every time I met with my friend at his house, he complained about how difficult this job was. He seemed stressed out over every little issue that came up.

Then, they asked for minor changes to how the tabulator function moved through the options. This is when my friend started making suggestions to me. He thought I was dragging this out because he just wanted the last payment for the work. I often explained to him that we only had a settlement once the deal was finished. These extra little adjustments were to be expected.

It had only been a few weeks since my friend and I started our Danish correspondence, which had to be translated into English and sent via email. Despite seeing the emails as proof that money had not yet been received, he still accused me of making him do work for nothing. His negative attitude was difficult to dispel.

It took me a few weeks to get the job done and receive my payment so I could tell him to leave me alone and that our friendship was over. We went from working together daily and spending time with each other's families on weekends back to nothing, all because of his greed and mistrustful attitude towards the business world. It was dismal, but a lesson I would learn many times in the future since, as an empath, I don't evaluate people based on their stories; I judge them by how they treat me. Growing up, I had reliable friends; morality was everything. Once someone betrays you without considering your feelings or emotions, you cannot return to a mutual understanding; you know where they stand.

## Bomb Scare

My friend and I visited Villa Park in Birmingham to watch the FA Cup semifinal between Liverpool and Wycombe Wanderers. His partner was a journalist for the Wycombe Press, so he scored us tickets right behind their supporters section. Having been a lifelong Liverpool fan, this was an incredible experience.

Unfortunately, Liverpool scored two goals in the second half, which made it difficult for me to remain impartial - I couldn't celebrate my team's victory, or I risked being beaten up.

To fit in with the other supporters, we acted as if we were cheering on Wycombe, and after they managed to get one goal back against Liverpool, the tension only grew.

I recall one person who came in late and took the row before us. A few minutes before the game ended, he abruptly stood up and left. It wasn't unusual, except he had a large box tucked under his seat when he entered. When he exited, the box was still there. In England, it was not unheard of for bombs to be planted at a football stadium, so my friend and I looked at each other with confusion and concern. We debated what to do next: leave immediately and tell someone on our way out, or alert those around us and risk getting stuck inside if it blew up. Then my buddy just said, "Screw it," and stepped over the chairs, pulled out the box, sat back down, and peered at me as if to say, "Let's check this out." Much to our relief, it was only 24 cans of soda. Strangely enough, he had been able to get past security with such an item! Regardless, we could sit back and relax while watching the remainder of the match. Go, Liverpool!

# Chapter 15

## Change is Coming

### 2002

On New Year's Eve 2002, my friends and I attended a fancy James Bond-themed bash. While most people wore black ties and elegant dresses, I decided to be different by donning a Russian camouflage military outfit with an oversized ushanka hat and army boots. We had rented a hotel room at the same hotel where the party was being held so we could retreat to our private space after the festivities ended.

We had more Cocaine than we could use, and every 15 minutes, someone wanted to go back to the room for another line. Nobody wanted to miss out, and our night became a routine of entering the function room, having a drink, and dancing with the girls- and then one of us would say, 'Let's go up to our room,' which was code for 'Let's have some more coke.'

Once the drinks were done, the crowd shuffled towards the elevators and crammed into our room. At least three people produced a bag of Coke to line up for those who wanted some. Thanks to my fiancé's brother, a major coke dealer in London, we never ran out that night.

Once the party was over, we had to find a taxi to take us back to one of the brothers' apartments. This proved complicated; we had blown through hundreds of pounds worth of Cocaine that night, but no one wanted to pay the set minimum fare of fifty pounds for any ride. So, instead, we ended up walking for two hours in the snow and slush, which had now become a watery mixture of both. We were all wearing fancy clothes, and the girls were in high heels, but it seemed too much to pay such an exorbitant fee for a warm ride home in such icy conditions.

Forget the excessive amount of Cocaine and the money spent throughout the evening, but paying fifty pounds for a taxi ride was pushing it.

∞∞∞

## 200220022002: A rare time indeed

### 2002 20 February 20:02pm

I learned after the fact that this was the day my fiancé and I broke up.

We had been planning a world trip for over a year. We had bought everything necessary, from backpacks to walking boots and everything in between, but never set a date or booked the tickets. When I asked her when to secure it, she hesitated and never confirmed. Until this day, when she finally told me she didn't want to do the trip, she had only encouraged the idea to keep me with her, but she wasn't going!

This was a massive shock to me, but one I had become accustomed to over the years, and from regular heartbreak and being let down by the ones closest to me, this hardly came as a shock, more so than just a knife in the back. Then, I would deal with the outcome, the only way I knew, and start again.

Given the situation, we ended things on good terms, or at least as good as possible. I moved into my friend's pub the following week, and he offered me a job to help him manage it with his family. She assisted me with the move, though it was more so she could get me out of the house quickly more than anything else.

It was only a few weeks later when I discovered that she had moved on to someone else, and then the nerve she had to come back and inquire as to why the computer I'd given her wouldn't start up.

When I walked away from the situation, there was an estimated 300 pounds that I owed her, but we had never kept a record of who paid for what and when. Since I had no one to turn to in this foreign country, I decided not to worry about it. Instead, I gave her a new large-screen television that I'd bought, a PC that cost more than 1000 pounds, and many other items without asking for payment. Rather than leaving anything outstanding between us, I wanted us to be even.

Naturally, the pettiness had to come out. A few weeks into our split, I got her call stating that the computer I left with her wasn't working at all and I needed to fix it. So I arranged to come around to look, being confident it was working as I had built it only recently, and it worked fine when I left.

I went to check the computer, which wouldn't turn on and when I arrived, her new man was there—pretending he was just a friend. As I inspected the computer, he demonstrated how pressing the round power switch wouldn't activate it.

This was the most significant moment in being dumped for someone else history when I showed him the little on/off switch on the back of the computer, and suddenly it powered up and functioned like a charm.

I said my farewells and wished him luck before departing and never looking back again.

I still had feelings for her, but she wasn't having it when I offered to help with her brother's new pub and suggested he hire me as the chef. She had already made up her mind that she didn't want me around. So, I decided to focus on myself and take my next steps in life, and this was not the first time I was left alone to fight for myself.

∞∞∞

## The Black Boy Inn

After breaking up with my fiancé and moving into the pub with my friend's family, I felt pretty glum. It had been pouring rain for five weeks straight. I didn't have a car, so getting around was a mission, and I left when one of the adults in the pub was going to town as it was an hour or more walk through the empty countryside roads to reach a shop.

At the Black Boy Inn, where I resided, closing time was nine o'clock, making it almost unbearable. The landlord's two- and three-year-old children were often used as weapons to wrap up the final evening customers. They would shuffle over adorably, then shout "Bye-bye!" and wave their hands right in front of the customer's face, showing that it was time to go.

We also had a regular couple we joked about - they were on the bigger side - and they'd arrive and start snacking on chips and peanuts. Then they'd sit down with other relatives and have a full three-course meal with all the trimmings - plus seven cans of diet coke each! We'd joke that it would be better if they just drank full-fat Coke instead - it'll taste better!

There was not much of an evening drinking session like the other pubs I came from, and you were lucky to see a girl my age, which would make you wish that they would hang around but rarely did.'

I got a few dates while living at the pub, but none really worked out to something serious and often was nothing more than a night out for drinks.

## The Guy With The Demon Tattoo

The atmosphere in the Black Boy Inn was oppressive as I was isolated in the bar, working with only two other customers, their gazes sending shivers down my spine. They were talking in low voices about England's recent elimination from the World Cup, and one of them had already imbibed too much alcohol, bragging that he could have scored that fateful penalty with his eyes closed. I dared to point out that it was a bit different when you were standing on the pitch with 60,000 spectators watching and half the world tuning in on TV, hoping for a win. His face contorted with anger, and hostility grew, as did the realization that soon fists would be flying. Then suddenly two new customers arrived.

A couple in their twenties stepped into the bar, the man's bald head glinting in the dim light, adorned with a demon tattoo covering his skull. He pulled his girl close in a loving embrace before they approached the counter. With desperation in their voices, they asked if there was anything to eat, and I told them about my simple offering - ham and eggs with chips. Delighted at the prospect, they sat together at the nearest table, sipping their pints of lager.

The two soccer fanatics slammed down their pints of lager in excitement, eager to relish their ordered drinks. The stocky gentleman with the demon tattoo flashed his girl a sly smile as he paid for the meal before hastily darting toward the lavatories. Only moments later, the rowdy one reemerged from the bathroom looking spooked; he frantically tapped his friend on the shoulder, signaling that it was time to go. They left at an incredible speed, taking off without so much as a single word. Behind their wake were two untouched pints, symbols of nameless dread and foreboding.

The demon tattoo guy grinned at me as he returned from the restroom, a sinister gleam in his eye. His girlfriend was waiting with her beer, the only two left in the pub. Intensely aware of their privacy, he motioned for her to begin eating. A silent understanding hung in the air as they both finished their meal. With a knowing glance, they rose and bowed out of the restaurant, leaving the questions of what happened in those sixty seconds in the toilet unanswered.

∞∞∞

## Midmorning Pikie Interruption

On a Saturday morning around 10 o'clock, I came down to the kitchen for a cup of coffee when the landlord/head chef asked me if I could go out to the back area and tell the guy outside that we weren't purchasing anything. Assuming it's a typical transaction like people coming to the pubs to sell kitchen knives or a new food supplier, etc., but No.

Groggy from lack of sleep and holding my first cup of coffee, I went outside and was immediately met with a fast-talking pikey asking me what I was buying without saying a word. Shaking my head, I said, "We aren't buying anything," he questioned that response, claiming that someone inside had told him to go into the back.

*Pikey (/ˈpaɪkiː/; also spelled pikie, pykie ) is a slang term which is pejorative and considered by many to be a slur. It is used mainly in the United Kingdom and Ireland to refer to people of the Traveler community, a set of ethno cultural groups found primarily in Great Britain and Ireland.

The atmosphere in the parking lot had become incredibly tense, and the pikie was convinced we were interested in purchasing something.

"What do you want? A TV? A DVD player?" he asked again, as I re-iterated that we weren't here to buy anything. His words suddenly took a threatening turn. "Where are you from?

"I replied, I'm from Denmark.

"Pikie." What do you mean, Gunmark? What's that? he accused me of talking nonsense.

By this point, a white van had turned around in the car park, come back around, and pulled up close to us with two more pikies, including an enormous figure who must have weighed 140kgs hanging out the driver's door window. He then repeated the question: what do you want to buy? I played dumb and foreign, satisfying them until they promised to return later. Thankfully, they never showed up again -

- however, we found out soon afterward that they had moved into a field behind a pub not far away and were causing all sorts of trouble.- fighting every night, scaring customers away, stealing whatever they could get their hands on.

Apparently, in England at the time, it was legal for them to enter an unlocked field and stay for 28 days before the police could move them on.

They would roam around looking for an unmonitored area to occupy for their temporary settlement so they could feed off the surrounding areas like a giant parasite before finding another host to feed on.

∞ ∞ ∞

## *Wembley, London*

I had the opportunity to meet a blonde South African woman at a nightclub in Henley on Thames. Though I knew this wouldn't be a long-term relationship, we enjoyed our time together. After I changed jobs and moved to Wembley, it became clear that she and her family were only staying there to survive. Her mother was the only one with residence papers, while her son and my girlfriend were residing there illegally. Eventually, their mother booked tickets for them all to move to Dubai with her boyfriend so that she could find work as a nurse to make money.

The daughter had been caught on camera speeding in her mother's car a week prior, and suddenly, they offered to let me have the car for free. It was a significant warning sign that showed how they treated me and where I stood—I wasn't new to being taken advantage of.

So, I agreed to accept the car, and they gave me the Transfer forms to prove the change of ownership. The mother filled them out, but when it came time to write down the date of purchase from me, she was nonchalant about it, like it didn't matter what she wrote. She chose a date that happened right before her daughter got caught for speeding -- a blatant attempt to make me responsible for the fine. It seemed funny but wasn't at all. I knew they were trying to pin it on me.

I told her it was alright and that I would submit the paperwork when they left for Dubai. I didn't actually hand in the forms and used the car for the next few months until it broke down due to a burned-out clutch. No harm done; it wasn't my car anyway, and from what they said, they had already moved on to their new home in Dubai.

Funny enough, about a month later, I got a message from the daughter, now in Durban, South Africa. She had run out of money and requested that I pay for the car her mother had given me for free to help her out.

But I never responded to those messages and didn't feel guilty about it at all.

The most memorable part of that relationship was when we spent our afternoons at the local newsagent to buy cigarettes and soft drinks. The owner, an older Indian man, had the longest ear hair ever seen and was always a big subject when we left, as most people struggled to hold in their laughs and comment about them.

The hairs were sticking out maybe 1 inch from the hole in his ears, and they had grown into such a dense bush that his whole ear looked like a small shrub just sticking out, and your eyes were forced to notice them.

∞ ∞ ∞

## The Chaotic World Of Surrey Cricketers

As the Head Chef at The Surrey Cricketers in Windlesham, I couldn't help but feel like I was living a real-life version of Fawlty Towers. The bar manager was an alcoholic whose relationship with the wealthy landlady was as puzzling as it was strange. I suspected she might have had a crush on him or owed him a favor from a previous liaison. Every night was just another opportunity for them to get drunk and show off to their friends. When I started, my second chef needed help to work independently and required constant supervision. He seemed like a good kid, but he had gotten himself into trouble in the past. This was his last chance to try and get back on track.

The third chef to join us was from Liverpool—a true scouser with a knack for getting into fights. He packed plenty of energy, always up for a good laugh and pint.

Once, we found a gray squirrel stuck in the bedroom upstairs; it ended up in my room. I asked Ricky, the scouser, to guard one side of my bed, then try to trap the tiny creature when it ran out. I poked it with a broom, and as planned, it ran to Ricky's end of the bed, where he had a box ready. When he saw the squirrel scrabble to jump up, Ricky made a high-pitched scream and leaped into the window frame—three feet off the ground! The squirrel escaped and ran down the stairs while Ricky clung desperately to the windowsill; so much for his gangster mentality, he would just grab it and take it outside.

It took several attempts before we could get the poor animal outside without disrupting service. Eventually, we managed to get back to work.

After several months, I finally gave the second chef a shot at running a morning shift alone. Everything was cooked and prepped when he arrived, so all he had to do was make sure the service went smoothly.

When I returned mid-service, one of the dishes wasn't right. It was supposed to be a chicken liver salad with a red onion pickle, but what he served looked like leftovers from an animal food bowl.

When questioned, he said he couldn't find the Red-Onion pickle. Instead, he decided to sauté some brown onions in malt vinegar and use it. I made him taste it, much to his strong protest, and he spat it out everywhere as it tasted just as bad as it sounded.

On another occasion, he called me in a panic because the local butcher had come by demanding payments for nearly seven weeks of meat that had been supplied to the pub. I told him to contact the bar manager, who had clearly neglected to pay these bills, and I wondered why the cuts of meat had gotten progressively worse lately.

In the kitchen, there was a joke which was used fairly often. When the waitresses came to take orders of freshly prepared food, a chef would hide a large bratwurst sausage in their pants zip and tuck it under the apron they wore.

As they went to grab the plate, They would say, "Wait a second," and then wipe the plate edge with the apron. They'd lift the apron just high enough for the sausage to show, then wait for the waitresses' usually embarrassed laughter or giggles before revealing that it was just a joke. This comedic moment they have led to great conversations when service ended and a funny icebreaker getting to know the waitresses and chatting with them after service.

One evening, I even cooked dinner for Brian May from the band Queen, amongst other famous people.

During my stay here, five of my closest friends from Denmark came to stay for a week and hang out with me. Upon arrival, I drove them straight to the nearest pub for drinks and conversation. This was when the hilarity began; when they decided to use the two-finger hand gesture used in Denmark (the back of the hand facing the bartender) to order their drinks, it created quite a stir until I could explain that this same gesture meant "Fuck you" in England. We had a fantastic start, and our old friendships strengthened as we went through more crazy days.

The only good thing about being stuck in a car for 5 hours when going to town due to a roadblock was the 3-day weekend we had at Newquay in south England, an area known for its surfing and partying.

We camped out and started the festivities as soon as we arrived, somehow finding ecstasy tablets and, after much searching and bargaining, a big bag of Cocaine.

We spent all night bar hopping and flirting with the ladies before ending one morning around 5 a.m., just as the sun rose. We were on top of the world!

We had strayed down a secluded dirt path behind the campsite when we stumbled upon a friendly horse. One of my friends started laughing as he pulled out the bag of Coke and joked that the horse's nostrils were so broad it could inhale the whole bag in one breath. We chuckled at the thought while ushering him away from the animal before anything unfortunate happened.

We stumbled across a massive flock of sheep behind some shrubbery. One of us - the same person who had devised the brilliant idea about the horse's nostril size - decided he would try to capture a sheep. He crept towards them in a low crawl on all fours, bleating out sheep noises.

We couldn't help but laugh at his attempt, as we all knew that sheep can be incredibly protective and may charge. But even if he managed to snatch one up, what would he do next?

He was slowly getting nearer and nearer to one of the sheep, all of us holding our breath in anticipation. We couldn't help but giggle at how this situation could quickly spiral out of control when, suddenly, a 4X4 flew through the gate of the field. The noise it made terrified the sheep away, nearly running over our friend in the process. Out came the farmer, screaming and shouting at everyone.

I was the only one who could talk to him, so I explained that our friend was intoxicated and we would leave immediately. But he became enraged, claiming he would contact the campsite down the road and take away our deposit. This posed a problem because we had made a 500-pound deposit there, but I assured him we didn't live there; we had visited after meeting someone at the campsite. He seemed to accept my explanation and told us to leave. We tried not to laugh too loudly as we walked away, in case he was watching us make our way towards the campground.

We would always smoke weed and drink after work but never during. I always had a strict rule to only smoke after.
One Sunday afternoon was quiet by 2 p.m.; typically, we would have under ten customers to feed between then and 4 p.m. and close.
So I agreed with the kitchen staff that we could have a joint while waiting and cleaning, as one of the boys had got hold of some top-shelf weed.
So we went down the back and started the joint and handed it around, not one puff in; we could hear a waitress call out, 'Check On," which meant a new order had come in and was hanging on the check board, we had another puff. We started laughing because it was some strong stuff. Then we can hear another 'Check On", we look at each other now feeling the effects. I tell one of the kitchen porters to run up and have a look, and that's probably just some serving of chips, and that's it.
As he runs up and a 'Check On" can be heard, we start panicking a bit, thinking, is it just the waitresses having a laugh, or what's going on?
Then I can hear the kitchen porter call out, "Chef, come here," followed by two more 'Check On" 'Check On," so we stomp out the joint and run to the kitchen, feeling pretty stoned. The panic has undoubtedly increased the effects.
We make it to the kitchen, where we have almost finished cleaning up. Most things are put away, as we expected no more

orders, but to our despair, on the checkboard hangs roughly ten tickets with large orders. We have walked into a nightmare because we are already behind. Hence, we start getting everything running again and meals prepared for coking when the bar manager comes in with four more tickets, saying hey, the local rugby team has just arrived. They want some snacks, like barbeque ribs, chips, filled potatoes, etc., for 40 people; I tell him we don't even have that amount of food as it is Sunday. We always try to get most food sold so we can start fresh on monday and prep again.

He looks at me in fear and says, I can't tell 40 rugby players they can't have food! So I tell him I will just cook up everything we have available and serve that, to which he agrees and tells them what food to expect.

While still trying not to look stoned and get 40 plus meals cooking, and snacks for the rugby players.

So, by now, we have got every gas flame lit on the stoves, and food is going everywhere to try and catch up.

I have called the kitchen porter in to help prepare dishes, and the second chef is getting them plated up as the food becomes ready; we are all fucked and can't stop laughing but trying to keep it going.

In the middle of this, the landlady pulled one of her wealthy friends into the kitchen to discuss how they would cook a crown of lamb with me. Still, I'm not in any mood for this drunken discussion and have meals going anywhere, so I have to politely try and tell them I will come out after and talk with them while not sounding too rude.

We managed to feed everyone in a reasonable time. Still, the kitchen now looked like something like a war-torn country. We had destroyed and used all the prep we had left, and no meat or anything was ready for the Monday shift.

So, with the cleaning and ordering new food, we left the kitchen at 8 p.m. when it usually would have been 4 p.m.

That was the first and last time we ever smoked during kitchen service.

This was also where I met my future wife. We moved to Australia not long after and got married. It must have been the Bratwurst sausage trick ;-)

The day she showed up with her travel companion, I locked eyes with her, and there was an undeniable spark. We had just completed our morning duties, so we had time to get to know the newcomers by having a few drinks with them before returning to work that evening.

Before the manager and the girls left in a convertible that belonged to the landlady (but he pretended it was his), I jokingly told my future wife that she would end up in my bed that night. Her response was a firm "no fucking way," followed by both of them bursting into laughter. With a beer in hand, they flew off with their hair dancing in the wind as the bar manager attempted to woo them with his driving skills in the silver Audi convertible.

Once my shift was finished, I headed to the bar for a well-deserved beer and to review tomorrow's food orders. There, I spotted the women had already arrived back and were having a good time. Knowing this was my chance to make an impression, I quickly joined them. We connected immediately, and the night stretched on with more beers until the pub closed its doors. I then walked her back to the staff residence a few hundred meters away.

Unfortunately, the door was locked, and she couldn't get back to her friend, who was likely already asleep or mad that we hit it off so well. This meant she had to return to my room and sleep in my bed, even after I had repeatedly warned her beforehand. She kept saying that nothing would happen but still replied with a "typical" under her breath.

Nothing happened that evening, although I certainly tried.

But I also knew the woman was staying in town and working with me for a while, so I respected her wishes and was in no hurry to catch the girl of my dreams. I was going to catch her full attention eventually.

∞ ∞ ∞

## Daylight Robbery

The Market Hotel in Reigate, London, was an unusual place to work as a Head Chef - only serving food for lunch and not on Sundays. The manager was paranoid, egomaniacal, and didn't care about the staff. The locals talked about how he had been robbed at gunpoint before and now carried an alert button around his neck to call the Police whenever pressed. At night, the hotel was like a fortress; no one could leave or enter without setting off the alarm. Since I couldn't access the alarm codes, I had to stay in my room, kitchen, and toilet facilities. One night, I had my girlfriend over; when she left to go to work, the alarms went off, prompting the manager to come running - he yelled at us for leaving the door open.

He didn't care much for me; it infuriated him when I won the competition hosted by the company that owned thirteen pubs in London.

At Christmas, the chefs would compete to see who could make the highest profits compared to last year's figures for each location. When I came out on top, I received loads of recognition from the owners, and a bunch of red and white wine was presented at one of the pubs. I gave those bottles away to all the staff.

He eventually got me fired when he learned that my girlfriend was expecting, and we planned to move to Australia in three months. He used this as an excuse for dismissal, even though I had informed our superiors about what was happening.

On my final day of work, due to the terms of my contract, they had to pay out a lump sum of 1200 pounds, including wages and holiday pay. He pretended not to realize it was that day and said he had no money available.

I demanded my owed money from the manager, and with some subtle hints of how the money could be extracted, he knew I wouldn't be leaving without it. He proceeded to frantically open cash registers and empty pokie machines of coins until he was still 60 pounds short.

Without protest, I snatched up the collection of notes and coins and headed for the bank next door.

The woman behind the counter raised an eyebrow at my bulging bag of money, then asked in disbelief if I had just robbed the pub next door. I told her 'kinda,' and then explained the whole situation.

She keenly assessed me before informing me that there was a 25-pound fee for converting currency at the bank, but she knew the pub manager and her own words; he was an asshole and decided to waive it, wishing luck to me and my new family on the way.

The same day I secured a chef job 30 minutes away, I started work in an opulent restaurant.

It looked like a lot of money had been spent on renovations, but the staff quarters were abominable. The walls were so old that you could have punched a hole through them, and mice ran unchecked even in our mattresses at night.

Knowing I'd only be there for a few months, I got to work to save up for my trip to Australia. One unexpected benefit was that some of the staff worked cleaning at a local jail and would receive confiscated weed from prison officers, which they'd allegedly secured by flirting with them.

Despite feeling guilty about the inmates getting taken advantage of like this, it certainly livened up our nights! I bumped into one of these co-workers five years later in Australia —we exchanged amazed greetings. We shared stories before going our separate ways.

After saving the money for my plane ticket to Australia and stuff for when I arrived, I had to lie and tell my job that I needed to go home to help my family.

I arranged to stay with a friend in the Victoria Inn in Peckham for the night, where she was working, before heading off early morning to Going Places travel shop in Ruislip, on the other side of London.

Despite leaving plenty of time to get there, some huge demonstrations caused delays on all the tubes.

I called the shop to let them know I'm running a bit late due to the demonstration, but I'll be sure to come and get the ticket. They tell me they will wait for me.

My train arrives at the station, so I dash three kilometers to the store, only to find it closed when I get there. No matter how many phone numbers I dial, no one picks up.

So I returned to the hotel and decided my best option was to try my luck at the airport in the morning since check-in began at 8 a.m. My flight was leaving at 9 a.m.--not giving me enough time to catch a train if I went into the store first.

The situation now rests on my shoulders and how I can make this work in the morning.

I get to Heathrow and explain my issue at the customer service desk. The lady was sympathetic and could verify that I had made a booking. Still, the ticket wasn't available for me to collect through them. I then tried calling the Going Places shop at 8 a.m. to ask why they didn't wait for me, only to find out the person I had spoken to wasn't in today. So, I inquired if they could have a taxi deliver my ticket to the airport, and I'd pay him upon arrival. None of the taxi drivers they spoke to would do it, so one of the girls offered to drive the ticket to the airport as long as I paid for her fuel. It was 8:30 a.m. and about a 45-minute drive. I returned to the service desk and explained my situation; she said she would check me in and try her best to get me an escort through the checkpoints quickly, provided I had a ticket. The girl arrived at 9:25 a.m., and I was filled with despair. I handed over my last cash for fuel, grabbed the ticket, and ran.

At the service counter, a woman looked at me impatiently and said, "Run!" I followed her through security, where we were quickly waived through—no need to stop and check our bags. We breezed past every other checkpoint until we were outside on the tarmac, where the plane had already arrived. I scrambled up the stairs, and as soon as I reached the top, they closed the door behind me, and the plane prepared for takeoff. The gods must have been smiling down on me as I began this next stage of my journey to Australia. The trip ahead of me was going to be my longest yet, and this was not how I had pictured immigrating to Australia would start, but I made it.

# Chapter 16

## Australia – Down Under

### 2003

Straight from the airport, we traveled to Jurien Bay on my first day in Australia. My soon-to-be wife and her mother picked me up from the airport and drove us 5 hours north of Perth to their home. We arrived at night, and I met my future father-in-law and the very welcoming locals. At the pub, they invited me out to go on a Cray fishing boat early the following day, which sounded like an exciting adventure. Late that night, I had several drinks and played pool before collapsing into bed.

At 4 a.m., I woke up feeling exhausted and wished I had said no to the boat voyage. As we left the harbor, the sky started to lighten up with the sun rising. Everyone was excited, but as we sailed further away from shore, my nausea began to increase until there was no escaping it—no hiding place or restrooms onboard—just constant rocking. It dawned on me— what seemed like an exhilarating journey earlier was just a big mistake and the jetlag kicking in.

I was hanging onto the side rail seated atop a plastic crate, sliding back and forth if I didn't grip it hard. The sun was now up, blazing down on my pale European skin. Because of this, I eventually got sunburned on the left side of my face, shoulder, arm, and leg. It felt like three hours of torture as I prayed to Neptune, the god of the sea, to end it all.

In addition to my sickness, exhaustion, and pain, the deckhands decided to be funny by sliding over a leopard shark from a recently emptied Cray pot they were unloading—shouting, 'Here you go, Danish boy!' as it snapped at my feet in sandals.

I could barely kick it away while also managing not to fall off or vomit on the boat's edge. After the horrid seasickness subsided, I witnessed incredible sights, like flying fish landing on the boat and several dolphins leaping out in front of it.

It's not quite how I expected my adventure to start, but certainly one I'll never forget.

∞∞∞

## Security Down Under

It took several months to apply for a visa and get marriage certificates, doctor tests, and several police clearances, as I had lived in 3 different countries. I needed to get them from Australia, which cost about $35 and took four weeks; the UK cost about $100 and took 12 weeks. And in Denmark, my mother walked into a local police station, and they printed it straight away at no cost.

I decided to get as much training and certificates in the security industry before I could work, so I was ready. I obtained certificates in security operations 2 & 3, Baton and handcuff usage, first attack fire fighting, bodyguarding, and emergency first aid. Before starting working, I wanted to ensure I was fully prepared. I was trained and certified in security operations, baton, handcuff usage, first attack fire fighting, bodyguarding, and emergency first aid. I was quickly given two job interviews once I had the okay to start to work. My first one was at someone's house for a part-time position on a security team in a popular nightclub. Another Guard and I stepped into the intimidating kitchen of an imposing figure with his shirt off and a gold chain draped around his neck. His associate hung nearby and just stood there looking tough. We opened the job manual presented to us and immediately knew it wasn't quite what we had expected. The uncreative presentation gave off an unprofessional vibe, with hand-drawn pictures of directions for hand signals and a bold proclamation that "the patron is always wrong." The real kicker was the picture accompanying the description of the hand signal for a female - a crude attempt at two hands cupped around two imaginary breasts. We finished politely and couldn't help but laugh once we exited. I still have the manual tucked away; it's one of the funniest things I've ever seen. Not surprisingly, we decided against taking either job - even the gig in a strip bar could have sounded more appealing. My companion, a tall English guy named Sam, let out a sigh of relief as we stepped outside and into the cool night air.

"So, what's next?" he asked, looking at me with a raised eyebrow. "I have another interview tomorrow," I replied, pulling out my phone to check the details. "It's with MSA security downtown. They're looking for security guards." Sam nodded, his expression thoughtful. "That sounds better than working at a strip club, that's for sure." We chuckled at that, and I felt slightly better about the job search. The nightclub was not the best fit, and there were much better possibilities out there. I then got hired by one of the more prominent companies in Perth, MSA Security, and started my journey. As we walked out of the intimidating house, I couldn't help but feel a little relieved that we had decided against the job. The manual was hilarious, but I didn't want to work in a place that didn't take their security seriously.

One of my first jobs was as a security guard for a Perth company. My manager then, arranged pre-screenings of popular movies before their release date.

As mobile phones had become able to record quality footage, film companies wanted increased security to prevent people from recording the movie.

We searched everyone with both handheld and airport-style metal detectors. All phones were confiscated and tagged with a receipt number so that they could be collected once the movie was finished.

This operation required many large boxes to store the phones and staff to watch them, leading to arguments about people being forced to part with their devices.

My next job as a Security Officer was for a large electronics store in Perth CBD. One of my duties involved theft prevention, and I often worked overnight shifts due to the multiple attempts at ram raids. One Security Officer would always be present if someone tried to break in so that I could immediately call for backup. However, one of the perks of this job was being stationed next to a long escalator that brought customers in and out of the store. On hot, sweltering summer days when women wore less clothing, we couldn't help but be thankful for the view we would have daily as the women in short skirts would leave the store.

## Crazy People & Bird Attacks

I had only worked in the high-rise for a few weeks at St George Terrace in Perth. Still, already, I felt like I'd learned so much and settled into my new environment. The central part of the building was the Magistrates Courts on several floors upstairs, which meant there were lots of people coming and going. One person in particular stood out: he was a middle-aged man with an impressive build but with scabs all over his face, chest, and arms. He said the marks were from stress, and he needed to be upstairs for a court case. Unfortunately, he wasn't on the list. All I could do was direct him to the court's reception desk upstairs.

So, I called ahead to let security know what was happening. Around 10 minutes later, he returned to the ground floor, escorted by security. He was furious that he couldn't go up for his court case. He began screaming and acting wildly as soon as he arrived; I tried to explain why he couldn't go up and offered to let him wait around if he calmed down. But when he started advancing towards me- I found myself behind a small marble corner desk with nowhere else to go- I knew it was time to act quickly.

Raising my voice and standing chest-to-chest with him, I got him to understand how serious this situation was: if he didn't calm down, I'd have to take him outside. Wrestling with McScabby covered in scabs wouldn't have been too pleasant either! Supposedly from stress, but I would take another doctor's diagnosis before being keen to wrestle with him, scrape most of these scabs off, and have them sticking to me! Thankfully, my warning worked, and he sat back down and left peacefully afterward.

I remember getting a call from the building manager, with whom I had a great work relationship over the two-way system, asking for assistance urgently on the roof of the building. My heart racing and questions swirling, I rushed to the roof. As I hopped through the door to the outside, I could feel something wasn't right. I felt like I was being watched and heard a giggling of some form, but I couldn't identify its source. Adrenaline surging, I burst out onto the top of the building, almost tripping over a support beam as I did so, and then turned to run away. Before I knew it, a large hawk swooped down at me from out of nowhere. Now, a door further ahead popped open, and the building manager, Steve, was calling for me to run for cover; as he was calling out, it got him as well.

We giggled and then ran for cover, but not before we had tempted fate a few times along the way when the Bird would drop from a building across the street and then disappear, but then glide over the edge of our building for an attack and you had to jump for cover.

As we huddled behind some equipment on the roof, the hawk circled overhead, screaming and flapping its wings. I couldn't help but feel amused at the situation: two grown men cowering from a bird. But in reality, the hawk was not to be underestimated. It was a fierce predator with sharp talons and a powerful beak.

Steve and I waited for what felt like an eternity until the Bird finally flew off to find its next prey. We let out a sigh of relief and then burst into laughter. It was a ridiculous situation, but one that had brought us closer together.

Afterward, we decided to head back inside and grab a coffee to calm our nerves. As we walked down the stairs, Steve turned to me and said, "You know, I've been meaning to tell you something. I've noticed that you've settled into your role here, and your quick thinking with that guy in the lobby impressed me."

I smiled, feeling a sense of pride. "Thanks, Steve. I appreciate that." We continued down the stairs, chatting about work and life, until we reached the lobby. As we walked towards the coffee shop, we noticed a commotion by the entrance of the building.

A group of people had gathered near the revolving doors, and there was an argument taking place. We made our way over to see what was going on and saw a man in a suit and tie yelling at a security guard.

"I don't care who you think you are; I demand to see the CEO of this company right now!" the man shouted.

The security guard, looking flustered, tried to calm the man down. "Sir, I'm sorry, but you can't just barge in here and demand to see the CEO. You need an appointment."

"I have an appointment!" the man retorted, waving a piece of paper.

We both moved over quickly to assist, and after a few minutes of tense negotiations, it appeared the gentleman had misread the official documents regarding his house mortgage being revoked and he was to be evicted, but today's date was not for him to attend; it was merely a notification of the impending eviction. The man, now calmer, as he had 28 days before the eviction would be executed.

He thanked us for explaining the situation better and made his way out of the building. Steve and I exchanged a look of relief and then continued to the coffee shop.

As we sipped our coffee, I couldn't help but think about the different situations I encountered at the high rise. From dealing with an angry man covered in scabs to being attacked by a hawk to diffusing a potential confrontation between multiple people, it was clear that there was never a dull moment. But despite the challenges, I loved my job and was grateful for the experiences it brought.

Unfortunately, my tenure in this job was only temporary since I was brought on to replace the permanent employee who had taken a month-long vacation. The management team was sorry to see me go when my time came up and offered that if they ever needed to fill this position again, I would be the first person they would call.

I was a security Officer for the West Australian newspaper for about one year. It was quite an intriguing job, as you got to meet a wide variety of people.

They would show up and ask to see one of the editors. However, when I informed them that they had no appointment or called up the editor in question only to be met with a stern "Do not let that person in," things could get interesting. The façade of politeness would quickly vanish and leave behind someone who was quite unpredictable.

A middle-aged man wearing a suit, who had a look of respectability about him, came up to me. As soon as I told him no, he started claiming that some mysterious leaders had sent him and they had proof in the form of pictures of spirits. At this point, I knew it was best to agree with him and get him out as politely as possible. One woman in the parking lot said she saw an angel floating from above, but nobody else could see it. She even asked them if they did, but nope - it was only visible to her. We had a regular informant who knew confidential information on some mafia associates, and he wanted us to provide protection for him in exchange for what he was offering. We could not give him such protection and tried to explain to him that if he were spreading the word about their affairs, then, of course, they would be after him.

He came by every week, although we weren't sure how much legitimately valuable information he possessed. One night, he showed up around two in the morning, banging on our door. I answered the intercom and heard him say they were after him again, but he ran away when we did not let him in. Still, he returned the following week.

During our shifts, we encountered many people suffering from mental health issues. We had to be the ones to facilitate their entry and access to the relevant services they needed.

The engine of my Ford Falcon Xr6 growled like a beast, ready to be unleashed as I drove on my last day before moving to Queensland. I had poured all of my hard-earned cash into this car, and the thought of getting rid of it made me bitter, but then I saw the glint of a Mitsubishi Lancer next to me at the lights. The other driver rolled down his window, challenging me with a smirk. I accepted without hesitation; this would be my last race before I said goodbye to my beloved vehicle.

The red light flickers and then switches to yellow. My foot slams down on the accelerator, and I'm off as the green light glows. The engine of my Ford growls like a wild animal, pushing me faster and faster as the Mitsubishi joins in with its thunderous roar. Pushing past one hundred eighty-five kilometers an hour, I look into my rearview mirror and see nothing but darkness, and the Mitsubishi is long gone.

Instantly, a burst of bright blue light pierces the night behind me. As I pull into the right turn lane at work, the police cars come into view, and now I know they're coming for me.

I could've sworn I was in the clear, but before long, they were on my tail, a pair of cops in a cruiser. The younger one was going ballistic, haranguing me about how fast I'd been going and claiming that they had been doing 140 Kilometers per hour and still couldn't catch up. I told him I needed clarification, maybe 80 or 85 at most.

He started to curse and examine every inch of the car for any violation, though it was clear they hadn't caught me on radar. The older cop was wearing an amused smirk; he seemed aware of what had played out. If they hadn't gotten a speed reading, they could do nothing. He explained that they had come out from a side road further down and only just managed to spot the Mitsubishi Lancer as it whipped past them.

The young cop handed me the ticket with a stern glare, condemning me with his eyes as he levied the relatively small fines—$150 and three points—on my driving record. I was amused; they would have taken my car away in the UK and thrown me in jail for this offense. So I happily accepted the punishment and waved goodbye to them, making my way to work, only a few steps away from where they had stopped me.

If I'd seen them coming just seconds earlier, I could have dashed behind the locked fence and escaped their sight. But it was too late; I was like a deer caught in headlights.

My manager was doubled over with laughter. He had been watching the whole spectacle play out on the security cameras. It made for quite an entertaining story to tell on our last shift together.

As I walked out of the building for the last time, I felt a sense of nostalgia wash over me. I had spent so many nights guarding this place, meeting a diverse range of people who came through these doors. But it was time to move on, and as I looked back at the newspaper building, I couldn't help but wonder what stories it would continue to tell.

As I drove away, I couldn't help but feel a sense of relief. No more late nights watching over the building and dealing with unpredictable visitors. Or so I thought. This was the start of a new chapter in my

## Queensland

We took a flight with our infant to Queensland, and I had arranged for our truck to be driven there in a bigger vehicle loaded with our possessions. This was the least expensive option —it only cost $1100—because not many items are shipped from Western Australia and back to the Eastern states; usually, stuff goes in one direction. My wife had set us up to stay at her aunt's place until we had found our own spot to call home.

It had sounded promising initially, but now that we were here and stuck living in a tiny sunroom with two adults and an infant, it was apparent this wouldn't be our permanent home. The other housemates smoked spots indiscriminately on the stovetop. The husband had taken to drinking heavily, and gambling on horse races--all of which made staying there for long seemed even more out of the question.

As the days passed, it became increasingly apparent that our extended family didn't quite know how to handle more people living in their house either. Small comments would be made about when we were planning to move. The hot water tap in the kitchen would be turned on when I was showering with the baby, and turning the water in the shower cold abruptly to remind me it was their house and not mine. It left me feeling unwelcome and uncomfortable.

We longed to leave, but getting an apartment does take some time. Though my job search was going alright, nothing was set in stone yet, and after a while, it seemed like life had gotten infinitely worse, and we were constantly fighting.

It had been maybe eight months since I'd last smoked, but here I was with two choices: drive away and chain smoke or fly into an unholy rage due to the relentless rudeness and insults. We felt powerless to escape the situation.

I had relocated to the other side of the world and ended up in Queensland, where nobody knew us, and we had no support besides those who wanted us out of their home.

When I asked a local support group for help, they could only assist my wife and kid, but not me. My wife didn't want to take that route, so we remained in limbo for a few weeks until luck favored us: we got approved for the rental place, and my job was confirmed. This happened in the nick of time before everything spiraled out of control.

We moved into our new apartment, and leaving the aunt's house was a significant relief. The place had two bedrooms, a living room, and a kitchen much larger than what we were used to, but it was perfect for our little family. We spent the first few days unpacking boxes and setting up our new home.

One evening, after we had put the baby to bed, my wife and I sat on the couch, sipping wine and enjoying the quiet. "I can't believe we made it," she said, kissing me.

"I know," I replied, pulling her closer. "It feels good to have our own space again."

We settled into a routine over the next few weeks. I worked during the day, and my wife looked after the baby and worked on her projects. We explored the city when we had free time and slowly felt more at home.

## Brisbane CBD Security

From 2004 to 2009, I worked as a Security Officer in Brisbane CBD for ADF Security.

Over this period, At one point, I was the only Officer trained and allowed to work at multiple of the most prestigious high-rise buildings in the CBD. These included Waterfront Place, AMP, Comalco, Riparian Plaza, and Central Plaza, the main center of the skyscrapers in the city.

These structures were my domain for five years, and I dealt with senators, high-profile lawyers & prime ministers daily.

Additionally, I had the pleasure of having actor John Cena film scenes in my office for the filming of the Marine movie.

They were filming many of the action scenes in our lobby and the outside area, so we got to see and meet a few actors and see how it was all done.

It was a hindrance to our work sometimes. When filming one scene, in particular, John Cena and his co-actor, Drew Powell, spent a lot of time at our security desk/office. We had to wait for filming to stop before running in, write notes on the computers, and ensure the lift access was running as requested. There were also many mundane tasks, but we would get in trouble if not done on time.

But it was an incredible experience, and we got to see them throw people through a glass window and blow up a car on the streets just outside our office, which made for some pleasant distractions from ordinary life and just walking the floors and checking the doors.

## Burglar On The Boardwalk

One night, I remember patrolling the outside areas and hearing strange noises from the boardwalk below. I leaned over and saw someone dragging two wheelie bins away from the Kookaburra Queen boats. I cornered him further down the boardwalk and apprehended him until Police arrived to arrest him as the bins had been filled with alcohol from the bars on the River Queen boats, and he was trying to move it away.

One Sunday afternoon, I received a call from the manager of the River Queen Boats informing me that they had recently fired an employee who was highly disgruntled and had threatened them with physical harm. I went to the pier to meet with the manager and pointed out the person in question. He was then told to leave the property.

I stayed around for a while to ensure he had left. Still, the pier was extremely crowded, with people enjoying the cafes and weather. Suddenly, I saw the man running back toward the manager. I rushed into the coffee club through a different door to intercept him. When he lunged at the manager, I grabbed him and pinned him to the ground with an arm bar while calling for someone to call the Police. He fought against my hold but eventually calmed down when he realized his attempts were fruitless. I walked him 100 meters to the street while keeping him in an arm bar.

When we arrived on the street, the Police had already pulled up in a paddy wagon on the other side. I pushed the pedestrian button with my foot. I waited for it to turn green before marching him over in an arm bar to the paddy wagon, which opened up so he could be put inside.

## The Man With The Red Tie

On a Saturday evening, two Detectives arrived and asked for help locating a person through our surveillance system; the Police had an agreement with us so they could come to request assistance if needed. I showed them the footage they were looking for and soon located the individual walking away from the Botanical Gardens and onto the boardwalk before entering Jade Buddha nightclub. The only detail that stood out was his red tie, which we used to track him down. The Detective on the scene reported that this suspect was wanted in connection with several murders; he would journey from his home in the Northern Territory, kill a homeless person, and then go out partying afterward. On this occasion, a murder had recently been committed at the Botanical Gardens, and based on this description of a man wearing a red tie, he was apprehended.

Thanks to our efforts, we may have prevented a potential serial murderer from claiming more lives.

## The Veggie Mercedes

When we first moved to Queensland, we were trying to get ahead and didn't have much money, so we would try and buy a car we could afford outright so we didn't have to be stuck with loan repayments.

We changed cars reasonably regularly because of this, as they were always old and needed repairs. Still, when I knew something expensive would come up, we would sell one car and get another.

One of the cheapest cars we ever had was the Orange Beast, the cheapest car to run, and insurance costs $27 per month, fully comprehensive.

1976 old school Diesel Mercedes 240D.

I used to get used vegetable oil from a McDonald's restaurant in Brisbane CBD, where I worked security.

I always talked to the delivery drivers and contractors during security patrols. I worked out a deal to get 100 liters of used veggie oil from the McDonald's fryers from the company that empties and replaces the oil for them.

So once per week, they would arrive and give the fryers a clean, empty the old oil, and replace it with fresh. This way, I would get all the oil I needed to run my Mercedes for the week for free.

The oil would come in 20-liter barrels, and once I got home, I would empty them into a 200-liter plastic container I had on a shelf in a tin shed.

This was connected to with a brass tap handle, which I had used knead-it to secure, and then into a piece of garden hose which ran into a 2000 micron filter which was sitting in another 200-

liter container underneath and then went back up into the top container after the filter running with a bilge pump.

The tap was attached about 5cm above the bottom of the top container, so after filtering for hours and then letting it sit for a few days, all the sediment was below the tap. I could extract 80 liters of pure vegetable oil, and the car would run on that almost every day, except if it got freezing, it would be too thick. I would have to unscrew the fuel filter, which is on the top of the engine, so easy to get to, and then empty out the veggie oil and fill it with pure diesel, enough to crank over and get going as if nothing happened.

These cars are workhorses known to do over 1 million km on the same engine. I kept our family driving for well over a year before I had saved enough money to buy a bigger kilometer car for us to use.

I ended up selling the beast to a friend for the same price I had purchased, as it was still in excellent condition and would drive like that forever.

## Big Mickey

One night, while working security at Waterfront Place, my colleague Big Mickey and I went to get coffee from the Coffee Club. They were generous enough to give us free drinks every day.

As we left the coffee club Mickey picked up an empty glass bottle and put it into the metal bin next to a round palm tree and flower stand. He stuck his arm deep into the garbage can, to avoid making too much noise and it smashing.

I had known Big Mickey for years and had never seen him run from a fight or confrontation. Still, when a colossal possum ran up his arm and leaped onto the palm tree, all 165kg of him jumped like I had never seen before.

At the same time, I was on the phone with a client who needed assistance. The shock of watching the scene caused me to drop the phone on the ground. Quickly, I picked it back up and assured them I'd be available to help shortly.

One day, as we patrolled Eagle Street Pier, we encountered a cyclist riding through the area. We informed them that cycling was prohibited in the area and asked them to dismount their bike. Instead of complying with our request, they became offended and started yelling insults at us. Fortunately for us, the person had gotten stuck in a crowd of pedestrians walking past all the restaurants.

As we slowly walked towards the individual, we could see customers in Pier Nine restaurant looking out with curiosity as this person shouted obscenities while leaning their bicycle on the glass balustrade running along the pier.

As I neared the guy, he pulled a massive five-foot chain from his backpack. He swung his arm back, ready to swing for my head, but Before I had time to react, Big Mickey (all 165kg of him) had snuck up and secured the guy's arms behind his back.

He asked what was he going to do with that chain?

With twenty people watching, Big Mickey had taken the chain away and pressed him against the Balustrades.

As I was about to call for backup, three police officers strolled up the boardwalk towards us. I quickly signaled them over, and they arrested the man after taking statements from everyone present.

Big Mickey had always been a hero in my eyes. He had a way of taking charge of a situation and making everything right. I couldn't help but feel grateful that he was on my side, especially during moments like these.

As the police officers escorted the man away, I turned to Big Mickey and gave him a nod of approval. "You're a real lifesaver, you know that?" I said.

He grinned back at me, his eyes twinkling in the dim light. "It's all in a day's work, my friend," he replied.

We continued our patrol, making sure that everything was in

order. As we walked, I couldn't help but notice the way that Big Mickey carried himself. Despite his immense size, he moved with an ease and grace that was almost mesmerizing.

We had many experiences together and always knew what we were dealing with; we had each other's backs no matter what. We shared a similar code of conduct: treat others as you'd like to be treated and stay loyal to your friends. Unfortunately, due to circumstances in his family, he moved back to Sydney with his wife. We had to part ways after years of being great companions without any questions.

Love you, Big Mickey

∞ ∞ ∞

## Muay Thai

I started my journey with Muay Thai by training and fighting at a few kickboxing and Thai boxing gyms. Eventually, I ended up at VALHALLA Muay Thai in Brisbane, Queensland, Australia. It made sense to me; being of Scandinavian heritage with the Norse Gods from Valhalla, it seemed an appropriate name for where I trained.

The gym was managed by a no-nonsense man who stuck to his word, so after around half a year of training, I was ready to start fighting. But when I did, I dislocated my shoulder in my first bout--I was so angry with myself as I knew I could have won if it wasn't for that setback. All my friends were there watching, and I wanted to show them I had what it takes.

I recall the altercation and my shoulder popping out of its socket. Thankfully, we had an experienced doctor and two men from my corner to assist us. Together, they managed to get my shoulder back in place without going to the hospital. Knowing I would have had to wait for at least three hours and there wasn't anything else they could do, I drove home and returned to the gym two days later. My doctor prescribed a routine of elastic band exercises, which I diligently followed.

I practiced these elastic band exercises multiple times during my day job, and it felt more robust in a matter of weeks. After six months, I was ready for my second Muay Thai fight and earned a TKO victory in the third round! That's when my journey began. Finally I'd achieved an Australian title with 19 fights and nine wins. I fought and defeated some of those who later became world champions and had my final match at 38 years old for a South Pacific title. The judges, who had over 20 years of experience in the fight industry, commented that it was one of the most brutal yet entertaining bouts they'd ever seen.

But my journey in the world of Muay Thai was far from over. After retiring from competition, I became a trainer and mentor to aspiring fighters. It was my chance to give back to the sport that had given me so much. I opened my gym, Karma Muay Thai, on the outskirts of Brisbane.

At the same time as i was starting the dojo I had been accepted to join as a Police Officer in Queensland Police Services "QPS", and had taking the tests etc, but the Dojo was thriving and thats where my heart really was.

I wanted to create a place where fighters felt at home, could come and train hard, and become the best they could be.

But also where everyday people could come in and feel at home.

No ego and no bullshit, just a happy place where we would welcome everyone and help each other to grow.

Over the first few years, the gym became known as the place to go for serious fighters. We had a reputation for producing champions, and our fighters were consistently ranked among the best. But it wasn't just about winning titles. It was about instilling discipline, respect, and a never-give-up attitude in our fighters.

## Security Firm

For a few years, two friends and I started our own security business. We got several contracts to look after some high-rise buildings on Wharf and Ann Street in Brisbane CBD.

This was a good little gig, but it took a lot of work, especially after hours and then the meetings, as I was the operational manager and had to see the clients regularly, all suited up to discuss ongoing works and new contracts.

The first problem started when one of the two got caught with 2 pounds of weed in the work car. My friend kicked him out of the deal for obvious reasons, but luckily he found it. Not a client or the Police, as it stank when you opened the doors. He had just forgotten he hadn't delivered it, and then I got left in the glove box in the Aussie sun, which wasn't the most brilliant move.

This was also his downfall as not long after, he got raided at home, and they found hundreds of vials of steroids, pounds of weed, plus cash confiscated.

We kept our business running, but after some time, it was just too much work for the money I was making. If I got a 9 to 4 job, I would get the same money in my hand as working every night, weekends, etc., and not have the late phone calls from the patrol guards and meetings during the day.

So I got a daytime job, which also fitted into my training schedule, in debt collections, which sounded like a great opportunity and would give me much more free time to train in Martial arts and with the family.

## Debt Collection

I worked for one of the larger debt collection agencies in the state, focusing on real estate and helping owners evict people who skipped rent or didn't finish repairs. Usually, 95% of our job involved tracking down a debtor and informing them of their debt and possible legal action taken if payments weren't started. The work was alright until I learned how grimy the industry can be; no one wants to talk to you when they owe money. The people I worked with were also suspicious because of this, so it created a very hostile work environment.

I remember walking in on my employer, searching through my trash bin, looking for information about the business. This same person had a public divorce due to an affair with another employee who left and established her own debt-collecting agency as competition.

Ultimately, it became hard to distinguish between the collectors and those being collected from.

My endeavors in Muay Thai started flourishing when the owner began sponsoring me. He attended all my fights and often purchased several tables for each event. This was an incredible help since fighters rely heavily on selling tickets and tables to generate income. When his guests accompanied him, I'd usually manage to sell over ten tables, with over a hundred people cheering me on!

It came to a head when I was unstoppable; four or five consecutive wins and knock-outs later, I was in line for my biggest fight yet: a state title bout I had been working towards for years. On the day of the match, 140 people packed into the tables filled with my supporters and probably 1,000 in the crowd, making up a massive gathering in attendance.

I had trained harder than ever, with sponsors supplying shirts for the entire audience. A new walkout jacket was made, and my entrance music was chosen carefully. But when the bell rang for round one, within twenty seconds, I'd dislocated my shoulder; both my opponent and I merely stared at each other while the ref waved off the fight. There hadn't been any action or hits made, so it ended in a no-contest.

Everything I had worked for seemed to vanish instantly as I stood in the ring, looking around while the doctor put my shoulder back into place. I remember wanting to keep going, but that wasn't allowed. Someone called out, telling me I needed to leave the ring, and everything went blurry afterward.

Everything I'd worked so hard for had been taken away instantly.

Even though I'd been dealt such a blow, I managed to stay committed and still had fights booked, so I kept training to stay on track.

After all this, the business owner where I worked also decided he did not want to sponsor me anymore - But he didn't tell me that. He ignored my requests to get tickets for the next fights, and soon after, he got the manager to cut off my sponsorship.

A valuable lesson learned: when you win, everyone is your friend, but when you lose, you get to see people's true colors.

# Chapter 17

## The Karma Name

### 2010

I had started my Martial Arts fighting career and wanted an awesome fight name. Still, as usual, I couldn't just settle for something everyone else was using, like The Dragon, The Terminator, etc. I knew I needed an intense fight name that would strike fear into my opponents.

Having something that reflected who I am or what is important to me.

I was now running a security firm in Brisbane CBD in the working part of my life. This evening, I was driving to some secluded warehouses in the industrial area of south Brisbane to check they were all locked and secure. It had been raining heavily that evening, so the air outside was heavy with water vapor. As I drove in behind one warehouse, I turned into a dark gravel car park, then, as if fate itself intervened, my gaze landed on a large red door spray-painted with white lettering that read "KARMA." In an instant, I knew this was the moniker that I had been seeking! The words seemed to come alive with meaning: for every action, there is an equal and opposite reaction! With newfound confidence erupting inside me, KARMA was born.

The strength of the identity came from the word itself. Great karma implied a story worth telling. I liked the philosophical implications: action and consequence, right and wrong, good and evil. And the description could be used with multiple iterations.

For every action, there is an equal and opposite reaction! Karma.

In late 2011, I got the opportunity to go and stay in Thailand with Sangtiennoi Sor RUNGROJ, "The deadly kisser," at Baan Muay Thai Camp, where Sangtien was the Kru, the Fight was booked for Boxing Day, 25 December 2011.

We stayed in a hotel next to the camp with Sangtien's family living next door. We had dinners together and visited a few sites while training twice daily. It was grueling training, but the weather was similar to Queensland's, so we had a great time and enjoyed the place. The first two weeks were just heavy training and trying to get on weight until my Fight at Rajadamnern in Bangkok. We were training with several current champions, including Moses Sangtiennoi, the son of Sangtien, who was a current S1 world champion, and Bua, who was a current Raja champion.

My opponent was a South American Nak Muay trained by Samart Payakaroon, another Thai legend in Thailand, having won both Muay Thai and Boxing world titles and was a famous singer and actor.

I remember the day of the Fight. We met with Samart in some back streets. People were flocking to see him and Sangtien as we stopped at a small café. When the owner was told I was fighting later that day, he shooed some young boys away from the mopeds so I could sit and "rest legs," as he said in broken English.

Come fight time, I had to get shorts from the lost and found as they didn't like my black shorts, so I used a pair of Blue with Gold trim from earlier fights. I lost the Fight on points, having had to cut a lot of weight. The weigh-in was the same day, so I couldn't get my rhythm going. My stamina was hurting, but it was an incredible experience. A small win was the opponent being carried out of the ring and, at the after-party, later still couldn't walk around.

A few days later, we attended a colossal Fight show called THAI FIGHT, held in the King Palace Gardens in Bangkok, with thousands of people in attendance outdoors. The main event was Australian Frankie Georgio vs. Buakaw Por Pramuk, which ended with a dominant win from Buakaw.

The Mongkhon (sometimes spelled Mongkol) is a headpiece exclusively worn by Thai boxers and not in the fight sports of neighboring countries. This protection is said to possess special powers that bring good fortune and defense to its users. They are traditionally made with rope and fabric by trainers or teachers at Muay Thai gyms and then blessed by monks before being given to fighters. A Mongkhon may contain the bones of an ancestor or the hair of someone close to the wearer, usually adorned with sacred amulets. Nowadays, one can buy them in specialty shops specialized in Muay Thai, but many traditional camps still weave their own.

The usage of Mongkhons dates back to ancient Thailand when warriors would wrap cloth around their heads and chant Buddhist incantations before battle. This custom has changed over time, particularly in Muay Thai contests. Before entering the ring, a fighter puts on a Mongkhon and carries out the Wai Khru Ram Muay dance. When the performance is complete, someone from the fighter's corner - usually a trainer or camp owner – takes off the Mongkhon while chanting a prayer. Today, this tradition is observed in Thailand and any place where Muay Thai is practiced.

The Team Karma Mongkhon, which we use for all our fighters, was purchased in Thailand.

It has been attuned to its powers of protection and strength through centuries-old rituals. Sangtiennoi Sor Rungroj blessed this piece at his temple by the local monks and, over the years, several other monks before fights, infusing it with spiritual guidance. It has an illustrious history, having been worn for all of our 400+ Muay Thai fights and houses pieces from my three children's hair, personal items from deceased family members, and several protective Takruts. Most notably included is a set of three Father of Muay Thai amulets — Brass, Silver, & Gold —

symbolizing Nai Khanom Tom's legendary prowess that lends truth to the superiority of highly skilled Muay Thai fighters. Fused with Tiger skin and fur, these powerful elements are embedded into this one-of-a-kind headpiece.

# Chapter 18

## Spiritul Growth

### 2012

This year, I started training on my own to allow my body to recover from a highly active year of combat. Additionally, we were expecting our third child. After a few months of solitude, I contacted a local gym that needed Muay Thai instructors and taught people here for the summer. Afterward, I shifted focus and taught two students at a nearby park for two months until NRG Gym hired me. We agreed on a deal where they provided me with a boxing ring. I paid them $3 for each student who trained with me, encouraging me and the establishment to bring in more customers.

Beginning in the first year, I had a thriving client base and eventually outgrew my place of business. After negotiations with a local Police Citizen Youth Club, I was allocated two rooms to provide more space for customers. By 2013, we had 13 fights and 10 wins – a promising beginning for a fighting gym.

The extra space at the new location meant we could expand our Muay Thai and fighting training program, and more people joined. By the end of 2014, we had 39 fights, with 22 wins. The following year saw 44 fights and 28 wins, and now State titles were being earned regularly. 2015, I also began promoting shows, hosting two successful shows at the PCYC, where our gym was located. As I looked for a new place to move into to have our own space and achieve our goals, I found an old church that fit perfectly for what we needed in 2016. There was enough room here to build two boxing rings.

The church had been abandoned for a while, and weeds were growing from the pavement cracks. The building was in a state of disrepair, with shattered windows and peeling paint. However, I saw its potential and knew we could transform it into the perfect space for our gym with some hard work and dedication.

It took weeks of blood, sweat, and tears, but we did it. We ripped up the old carpeting, replaced it with new mats, installed new lighting, and painted the walls. I hand build a giant Karma Shark logo to fit up high in the middle of the room for everyone to see when you walk in. The shark symbolizes the Dojo being on the bayside and the main predator of the ocean.

We brought new equipment, including punching bags, weights, and resistance bands.

As word of our new location spread, more and more people started coming to our gym. We had fighters of all ages and skill levels, from kids just starting to seasoned professionals looking to hone their skills. And I was there every step of the way, pushing them to be their best.

As time passed, I began learning the downside of helping people. People were always grateful for my assistance, but when it came to me asking for help, they made excuses or refused to reciprocate the favor. It wasn't their job, they said.

Not long after, I got an offer to lease the minister's house next door to my gym, which was perfect. It made sense to live and work in the same place. This space was tailored just for us: even the former baptismal pool was converted into a steam room that could hold ten people comfortably. This benefited the fighters who needed to cut weight before fights and members looking to relax and detox after an intense training session.

This was the year I began hosting and managing my professional Muay Thai fight shows. The inaugural event was held at one of the most renowned spots in Brisbane, the Sleeman Centre.

The theatre holds up to 1200 people and offers an exquisite

Colosseum-style experience for fighters and spectators alike.

The show was an incredible success, making it the talk of town for months to come. I didn't make much money from this promotion, but it put my name on the map.

The 4th edition of PMC was scheduled at a new, smaller location. The prices for the last spot had skyrocketed, and I needed to switch things up to make some money. We picked a nearby venue with a capacity of just 500 people. However, we still put in the same effort and attention to detail. All fighters who participated using full Thai rules were paid a fee plus a portion of ticket sales as an incentive for them to give their best performance in the ring. Additionally, Yokkao agreed to be the event's official sponsor and provided gloves, canvas, merchandise, and international coverage.

Right before the event, something happened to mar our relationship; I had to separate from Yokkao since false details about the show had been presented to them, and they would only agree if I met new terms. Oddly, a person from my inner circle was speaking with those same people in Thailand, which gave me clues about potentially unethical behavior.

I had been sending fighters to his center every week so they could refine their techniques and we could both develop our businesses. He was supposed to prepare them for their fights, and I would reimburse him for his time as an exchange.

He had taken the chance to put his nefarious plot into motion: a revolt stemming from jealousy of my triumphs.

I felt that some of my comrades had been converted, never giving me a clear response when I inquired about their fidelity. Therefore, I planned to talk with one of them at my gym. However, he ran off before I showed up 30 minutes beforehand.

I sensed something amiss on the day of my last fight show, December 16th, 2016. Still, I pushed on with running a successful event, which took priority to ensure all the competitors were looked after and the crowd had a good night.

Then, in the next few days, some of my fighters vanished without explanation. But one morning, they returned in the early morning, grabbed their trophies and belts before anyone knew they had been there, and then left like thieves in the night like nothing ever happened before anyone knew they were there. Shortly after, my former friend opened his new gym, filled with many people I had trained. These individuals displayed no respect or decency for anyone and saw nothing wrong in exploiting another's good deeds. Seeing them take advantage of me without any thanks or acknowledgment for my help when they had succeeded was disheartening. These people acted like cowards rather than showing courage and confronting me about their grievances.

Some I had pulled from drug abuse and gave them homes and chances- all of which were cast aside without hesitation because it was easier to avoid facing what they did instead. People need to be real, take responsibility for their actions, and communicate with their friends if things get hard instead of pointing fingers and running away.

Despite the betrayal of some of my former students, I refused to let their actions hinder my progress. I continued to work hard and push my fighters to their limits, determined to show them that true success is earned through hard work, dedication, and respect.

We achieved more wins and titles in just six months than any other time and my dedication was rewarded when I was named in running Australia's Trainer of the Year.

As the years went by, my gym continued to grow and evolve. We hosted more successful shows, won more titles, and brought in even more talented fighters. I always kept sight of my goals and remembered the lessons I learned from my past experiences.

Reflecting on those events, I realized that my gym was more than a business. It was a place where people came to improve themselves to learn discipline and respect. And while some may have taken advantage of my kindness, many left my gym as better people than when they first entered.

I continued to push myself and my fighters to be the best we could be. We participated in more competitions and won more titles. And through it all, I never lost sight of what was truly important: helping people.

Eventually, I realized that my gym had become more than just a place for fighters to train. It had become a community where people could unite and support each other. And I realized that this was what I had always been striving for.

A healing station for the broken and a place to stay in a positive vibration of love for the strong. As I sit in my office, looking out over the gym, I am filled with pride and accomplishment. I have helped so many people over the years. I know that my gym will always succeed because of the moral codes we run by. A happy environment and strong people with good morals will always stand above the rest.

In 2017, there were 46 battles and 32 victories, signifying we were on the right path.

The following year, we had to relocate due to our old spot wanting to renew our contract for only a three-month window, which was outrageous for a business of our size with that much equipment and a hundred members.

So I found this new establishment five minutes away from the former location and close to a train station—it worked out perfectly.

We got the move out of the way over a weekend and set up our new home. My family could stay upstairs, which was great for reducing rent costs. However, it needed to be more sustainable in the long term. We had to constantly distinguish between work and home life, with people coming around at all hours. Furthermore, taking a break from work was hard when it was just a few steps away. We decided to relocate further from the gym so I could have some separation between work and me-time.

After a while, the chance to lease a shed next to our property arose, and we took it. This allowed us to expand our gym space and fit in a full-sized boxing ring for classes and the outdoor area I had built. Although this did cause some financial stress, the additional members we gained offset the costs. By the end of 2018, we had 59 fights with 25 wins, multiple titles, and the team was running strong.

The following year, we kept working as usual, with students joining and leaving at the same rate. We had a total of 47 matches with 24 victories. 2019 was going smoothly until the Corona virus pandemic hit, wreaking havoc on small businesses - most notably in the fitness industry.

# Chapter 19

## The Skill Tester

### 2020

At 4:15 p.m., I received an urgent phone call from my son. It was the middle of class time at the gym, and I had a full schedule ahead.

He told me that my youngest daughter had got her arm stuck in a skill tester at the local shopping Centre while waiting for mum to finish shopping.

My son and daughter had gone outside the shops and tried their luck on a skill tester/ claw machine, where several prices were up for grabs.

On their last try, he managed to grab onto a POP figurine box, which then got wedged in the winning area.

My excited daughter quickly put her arm in to give it a nudge down, only to find she couldn't move it back out again.

A small trap door inside the machine slides shut when pressed; this is what stopped my daughter from freeing her arm.

The phone call I received was in a state of panic because they had informed Centre management about their predicament but were left waiting for 10-15 minutes with no help. He said it felt like the people in charge didn't know what to do and couldn't get in contact with anyone. I told him to stay put and that I was already on my way.

I quickly told my staff what was happening, grabbed two tools - a chisel and a power drill - and raced to the shopping Centre. Upon arriving, I saw quite a crowd gathered around the Claw Machine and an inexperienced security guard still on the phone. My first question was why they hadn't called for emergency services yet when they were right across the road and would arrive within minutes. The manager's attitude shifted as she scolded me for raising my voice; she claimed they had done all they could to assist. This seemed hard to accept since they had yet to call for the emergency services or obtain the keys for the machine, which they don't have anyway, and must ask the company that operates the machine to provide them. However, their only option for doing so - a mobile number printed on the side of the machine - just kept ringing out.

Once my wife assured me that our daughter and she were safe, I began working to unlock the machine's door. The manager argued that I'd have to pay for damages, but her words fell on deaf ears. After a few minutes of tinkering, I unlocked the machine's main door. It was then that I noticed the trap door and the locking mechanism. When you win a prize, a small compartment opens up. Still, it had a locking mechanism that prevented it from opening again. My daughter had tried to pull her shoulder and arm back out but was unsuccessful because her elbow joint was lodged underneath, which wouldn't budge.

Luckily, emergency services had been contacted and arrived within 50 minutes of my child's arm becoming stuck in the machine. However, this could've been much faster if the staff had proper training.

It took another 10 minutes or so for them to dismantle the lock and release my daughter. I held her hand and comforted her during this time, determined to ensure she felt safe.

I gave her a huge hug, and I gave her the prize they had won, which I had picked up while dismantling the machine, and we were on our way home after a very stressful event.

But it doesn't stop here.

The following day, I contacted Center Management, explained what had happened, and asked what our next steps should be. Unfortunately, instead of an apology or guaranteeing that the incident would not happen again to another child, I received a simple "What are you going to do about it?" This prompted me to exhaust every option available to me.

I narrated my story, attached a picture before posting it on any local Facebook group I could find, and forwarded it to news desks and organizations like 60 Minutes and Occupational Health Services. Another strange coincidence was you saw these machines shut down everywhere with out-of-order tape because of COVID-19 and not to be used, but not in this center.

My efforts were met with success as people from Europe had seen the post on the news, and several media organizations started calling me for interviews. In addition, Facebook was flooded with comments - some criticizing me for teaching my daughter to steal, while others made threats of violence - but the post quickly went viral.

Soon enough, Channel 9, Channel 7, and a magazine published stories based on my daughter's experience, and shortly after that, the machines were removed.

Likewise, other parents shared their accounts of similar experiences they had been through with their children in those same stores.

So when someone tells you, "What are you going to do about it?" when your daughter has been wronged and people won't look after her.

I do whatever I possibly can!

For a long time, we were barred from operating our gym, and when we could, people needed to be masked and had to stay six feet apart. If one individual got infected with COVID-19, the gym shut down, tearing families apart due to lost revenues. I didn't believe in the agenda being forced on us. Still, I kept running until government pressure forced companies that collected gym fees via debit cards to close their accounts. This resulted in all of my business accounts getting closed instantly in early 2020. Soon after, I could not pay any bills: leases for rent, cars, mobiles, loans, house rent—all of it gone without warning since I no longer had any money.

The pandemic had caused my gym to suffer the most, not only financially but also emotionally. It was hard to see all of my hard work come crashing down in a matter of days. But I refused to let this defeat me. I refused to let this pandemic ruin everything I had built.

With the help of my family and some loyal friends, I managed to keep the gym afloat. We offered online classes and sold merchandise to our dedicated members.

For several weeks, I was facing a difficult battle. So, I reached out to all of my gym members with a message about the situation, saying I would accept whatever they could afford to pay into my bank account to express their satisfaction with our services. As another form of income, I even resorted to renting out some of the gym equipment.

The next step was to paint all the windows black, ensuring no one outside could see in. I also created 'the Karen wall,' two walls that measured 2.2 meters tall and 3 meters wide, which could be rolled out onto the driveway to shield the gym from anyone passing by, which allowed us to keep our activities private and keep track of who was coming in.

Many people were quite excited to take action against those who refused to wear a mask and disregarded safety protocols while continuing to conduct business to provide for their children without any hesitation.

It was difficult for everyone, but I knew we would get through it together. And we did, slowly but surely. We started to see the light at the end of the tunnel as restrictions eased up, and we were allowed to open our doors legally again.

The COVID-19 pandemic revealed the ugly truth about our society and those willing to cling to any shred of power they had. They showed no mercy in calling the Police on their poor neighbors and friends simply because they had bought into the government's false agenda.

It was a nasty time for humanity that exposed how easily people can be misled. Some individuals followed the regime blindly, hiding behind masks. In contrast, millions of others suffered, allowing them to discard their values and betray those closest to them.

But through all this, my gym remained a safe haven for those seeking refuge from the madness outside. We had become more than just a training ground for fighters. We were a community of like-minded individuals who stood together in the face of adversity.

As we slowly began to rebuild and recover from the pandemic, I promised myself and my gym members - that we would come out of this stronger than ever before. We would continue to work hard and push ourselves to be the best we could be in the ring and in our personal lives. And most importantly, we will always remember the lessons we learned during this difficult time.

As we reopened our doors, it was clear that the world had changed. But inside the walls of my gym, everything felt familiar and comforting. The sound of gloves hitting punching bags and the smell of sweat and determination in the air was like coming home.

And as we welcomed back our loyal members, I couldn't help but feel grateful for

The vaccines appeared to be the saving grace of those already scared and triggered by not everyone wearing a mask or wanting one. People who refused vaccinations were labeled as some of the worst humans alive. It's humorous how it has changed now that we all know it was a scam. Those who stood behind the mandate of masks, shots, and total control look foolish now, with heart attacks, pericarditis, and unexplainable illnesses while people drop like flies. Most of these individuals still can't admit they were duped into believing this whole thing and can't put two and two together why this is happening.

By late 2022, we were running at full speed again, and I had learned more lessons that could have taken down more remarkable men, but I didn't quit.

During the pandemic, I helped many people with advice on surviving these restrictions. I also let multiple people stay upstairs at my gym as they couldn't get a place to live, or they had been kicked out because of loss of income, etc.

I also had numerous trainers employed, even though our income was suffering. Still, I had made a promise to them to keep paying. We would keep pushing forward so we could beat this crazy thing. Some weeks, I had to pay wages out of my own money because the business account was empty, but I did this happily as my staff had been made a promise. When you help people and give them good energy, it returns.

This created a new scenario for me, as I did all this to help people, and the more time went on, the more people would take advantage of my generosity. They did not pay rent, which was cheaper than anywhere else they could find; they had free WIFI, water, and electricity, but even this wasn't good enough for some.

The several people my friends recommended turned out to be drug addicts, which I then had to deal with and evict from the house. This caused significant stress on me and my family, as it could be constant drama, and I would have to leave home sometimes in the middle of the night to fix these problems.

During the few years of COVID-19, I housed 20+ people as they were stuck in all kinds of bad situations, and all came recommended by friends.

And less than five left on amicable terms, and we are still talking. The rest were booted out in many different ways.

Also, I'll mention that this was a commercial property, so no rental laws are applicable, and it's up to me who stays and goes. And let's remember these people were given help when they needed it the most, didn't pay a bond, got cheap rent, and some couldn't even clean up after themselves.

## *The Evicted Ones.*

Some were just on the day, pack your shit up and get out.

Then you had the ones digging in a bit harder and had to be physically removed.

One was told to move, but the weekend came along, and nothing got moved. The door was locked, and I could hear them smoking bongs and drinking, so every time I saw them, I would ask how the move was going, and they would reply that they were waiting for a friend to come with a car.

The car never came, and then by Saturday, after multiple requests to start moving, they were now waiting on a trailer.

Sunday came, and no trailer had turned up. I could hear them smoking and drinking still, and nothing getting done. so I got in touch with a friend, borrowed his mini truck and proceeded to park it right outside the stairs leading down from the gym, then went up and unlocked their door and advised them that we were moving right now, the truck was ready so they could start carrying stuff down.

This took them by surprise, and the move got started and was done within an hour. I dropped them off at their new place, and that was that.

The trickier one was a guy who had gotten hooked on Crack, so he became quite unstable and had threatened other people with a knife before. He made creepy comments about them, and his mind regularly made up stuff.

I again gave him several weeks' notice to leave, but he thought he could stay. When I turned up for him to move, he tried to hand me the rent money. I just said nah, mate, you need that for where you are going and leaving this weekend. This was a Friday, and I emphasized that he was moving out no matter what.

He still hadn't moved by Saturday, so I asked him again. He said he had nowhere to go, so I got hold of a men's lodge advising they had one room available. They could take him straight away, as long as he called and arranged it and paid the bond, which was very similar to the rent money he had just shown me, so I gave him the details and told him to get this sorted, and he had until Sunday to move out and if he needed any help just let me know, and I would drive him there.

Sunday came, and he hasn't moved.

I knocked on the door, but there was no answer. I asked some people there; they had not seen him come or go out.

I knocked again, but nothing; I knocked even harder, but still nothing. I knocked for a third time and said out loud. Listen, if you are there, I will get the spare key and open the door.

I returned with the key and opened the door, and to my surprise, he was sitting right in front of the door and looking at me. I quickly looked around the room and saw he hadn't packed anything. He is holding a knife and cutting something with it, but he also has a larger blade on the desk next to him, so I'm on alert mode and will approach this slowly.

I asked him why he hadn't packed anything, and he replied he wasn't sure and if he couldn't just stay. I advised him again that this wasn't possible anymore as he had threatened other people in the house and made them feel very uncomfortable being there.

I slowly moved into the room, started picking up a few things, and said, "I'll help you. Let's get something packed now, and then we can call the lodge.

He moved his chair out of the way so I could get in, and I casually packed the larger knife when it was in reach and then moved towards the table where he had put down the other blade. After a few boxes were done and both knives had been taken away, I kept talking to him and explained what I was doing. Then I pulled down the bed sheet he had hanging as curtains so the light could enter the room. I also wanted it to start getting a little more uncomfortable for him so he would begin to realize the seriousness of the situation.

Once the curtain came down, he seemed to wake up from his drug-infused state and looked around and stated that he thought he better go for a walk now, so it was working! He became a bit jittery, and I told him no problem, I'll pack these boxes, and then we could get it finished.

He walked out without saying much, and then as soon as he was out of sight, I called a few of the other boys into help and told them to lock the door and help me quickly to get everything in boxes, and we would store it downstairs under a marquee which was just outside the front and would provide cover for the boxes. Then once this was done, I screwed the door off its hinges. I hid it in another room in case he somehow found a way back in, and then he could lock the door again.

I advised the others to keep all the doors locked, and if there is any sign of him, let me know.

He roamed the streets for a few days, and then I realized he had just been sleeping under the tarp we had put over his boxes, as I could see cigarette buts and a few cans of beer there in the morning.

I had gotten hold of some friend of his through a brother, and he said he would come and pick up his stuff a few days later, and then once this was gone, we never saw him again.

I heard he had been on a big crack binge and just hung out at the local pub with no shoes and cuts on his feet, and when he attended the doctors, they arranged for him to get some psychiatric help.

Another person I kicked out came back after some time. He was apologetic and asked if he could use the weights a couple of times per week and then start slowly training again. He seemed sincere, and I let him train.

He explained he would get paid on Wednesdays so that he would pay me then for the training, and if he could grab a pair of gym shorts now to train in, he would pay for it all Wednesday. I agreed with this and handed him a pair of shorts.

We both worked out and engaged in a good conversation about how he had come out from jail and just wanted to stay straight. He looked clean and seemed in good spirits, which gave me hope that he was trying to turn his life around.

As he left that day, I couldn't help but think he deserved a second chance at living an honest life - But I needed to keep an eye on him moving forward.

It was three hours later when I received the call from the Police. They had a man wearing shorts with my gym logo at the local service station. Their cameras had caught him filling up with fuel and then driving away without paying. I took off in my car to search all his known hangouts, but either he was gone or hiding well — I couldn't find him.

It had been at least three weeks since we'd last seen him, but then, he casually strolled down the driveway to the gym one afternoon. When I got the notification from one of the boys who lived upstairs that he had just arrived, I was at the far end of the driveway. And he was wearing my shorts, looking like he'd never left.

I couldn't believe it. After everything we had been through, the theft, the lies, and the deceit, he had the nerve to return as if nothing had ever happened.

I stood there in disbelief as he walked up to me, smiling, reaching out to shake my hand. I could feel the anger and frustration boiling inside me, but I kept my cool.

So I stick my head out and call his name, and he walks towards me as if nothing has happened and just says," hey mate, how's it going" So I ask him what the fuck he means because I'm pissed off, and he fucked up the last time he was here.

He claimed not to know what I was talking about, so I refreshed his memory about the shorts, not paying for fuel, being on camera, etc.

"You can't just waltz back here and expect everything to be okay. You stole from me and lied to my face. I gave you a second chance, and you blew it," I said, my voice getting sharper.

He claims it was a misunderstanding and had simply forgotten to pay for the fuel. I reply that I'm no longer falling for his excuses, telling him that he better turn around before things get ugly. He presses me for an answer, but I stay firm: if he doesn't leave, the next thing will be me taking a swing at him.

He acted like he didn't understand, so I hit him in the chest with all my strength. He buckled over and groaned before stepping back, then held his hand out with what he owed me. I forced his hand shut and told him he needed the money more than I did. I said he should use it to pay for the fuel he had stolen and never come back.

As he starts to walk away, he asks if he can return in a few weeks. I gave him a firm head shake "No," and told him not to return. He scuttled out of view quickly, and I didn't see him for two months until I ran into him at the local shops. As soon as he spotted me, his eyes dropped to the ground, and his demeanor changed—he was obviously avoiding me.

By the middle of 2022, business at my gym was running smoothly, but a few months later, my lease would end, and I was still waiting to receive word from the Landlord about re-signing. This was causing me great stress as I could not just pack up an entire gym on a month's notice. Even if I managed to find another place to rent in time, it would mean shutting down the gym and losing my primary source of income for my family.

Despite trying to contact the Landlord repeatedly, he has yet to give me a straight answer. He danced around my questions and avoided committing to renewing our lease. As a result, I had to take matters into my own hands and start looking for alternative places in our price range and size requirements.

We hadn't found anything within our price range that fit our needs, so I kept an eye on the market and checked in with the Landlord, but there was still no luck. The Landlord then began to do things that made it seem like he may be planning to sell the place without telling us until it was too late.

One morning, I received a call from another business on the same street informing me that they had noticed a real estate agent at the gym taking measurements of my property. He'd been back a couple of times during the week.

I quickly dialed the Landlord, who denied any involvement in this, a statement which seemed to be false. After all, it's not likely that a real estate agent would go to someone else's property and start taking measurements without the owner being aware of it and several times the same week.

Confirmed in my mind I was desperately searching for a new spot to move the business. We visited a few locations, but none of them were appropriate--the wrong size or in the wrong place. One morning, however, I refreshed the leasing website and came across the perfect spot--it was the correct size, had a reasonable price, and was only 5 minutes away from where we had been before.

As soon as I called them, I set up a viewing appointment and met with the agent an hour later. This place was exactly what I had been hoping for—the ideal location near transportation hubs such as the train station, freeway, and a college where many of our students originate from. I quickly gathered all the documents necessary and signed a new lease by the end of the week.

Boom, a new beginning in an upgraded location was in the making. I was ready to move away from all the bad vibes that had taken control of the former gym because of all the people constantly moving in and out. This meant clearing up those negative energies and replacing them with new positive ones, bringing back the dojo-style gym, creating a safe community where everyone wants to learn and grow together, and keeping away all toxic elements that could jeopardize our vision.

From all the battles I had been fighting since leaving Denmark trying to make a life for myself in England and now here in Australia, an ongoing struggle with people pretending to be friends, but in reality, they were just friends of convenience because it suited them. When the tables got turned and I needed help, they disappeared.

A funny thing was then the Landlord called about four weeks before the lease ran out and said he thought he would send that lease to sign. I told him he had dragged this on so long that I was looking elsewhere, but he was welcome to send it through, and I would have thought about it.

His reply showed his true intention. He told me that's "fucked up," and I could just get fucked and look for another place, and then hung up on me.

Again, when it suits them, they are all friendly, but when you stand up for yourself, they turn on you and disappear.

You know, when they can't debate and discuss a subject professionally without attacking or making up excuses, they are lost in their toxic vibration. Nothing you can say or do will help them.

## My accomplishments

I have brought up three amazing kids, the oldest being 20, who came out as transgender at 14 in high school. He was born a girl but always showed signs of being a boy.

But it was not until he started high school that he learned about himself and had the courage to tell me, his father. It was hard for me and him, of course.

But for me, because of the guilt, I felt, if I could just have helped him earlier, I was so proud of the strength he showed, with the bullying he went through and just toxic and evil children who can hate on others through social media now they can hide behind the screens.

This all went on at the same time that was mentioned in an earlier chapter when my close friend through seven years betrayed me and encouraged the students and convinced them to join him in trying to destroy what I had built from scratch with my own hands. That was a challenging year, and this all went on, but the strength I saw in my Son, was what spurred me on as well showing the haters who would come out on top after this was done and the dust had settled.

I'm still here and doing better than ever; my son is a pillar in the local community and loved by everyone. He works full-time as a special needs school teacher's aide and helps me run the Dojo daily.

He even has his own group of parents from the school who bring their kids to see him once a week and train with him because they love him that much.

My middle daughter has grown into a super polite and caring person who knows what friendships and family are all about, and she shows that every day. I can't wait to help her grow into a strong, independent, and successful woman soon.

My youngest daughter, having been diagnosed with Autism and ADHD, is one of the most loving and caring humans you will find, from her skills with computers and animations to how she has become an animal whisperer. I have no doubt she will be more successful than me once she grows older and can use all these beautiful skills to show the world who she is.

My wife, by my side, after 20 years, with our ups and downs, but still a team, you should be proud of the family you have created and the kids you have raised.

This is only the beginning of the Karma story, until we meet again in "The Awakening".

It has only just begun!

Remember, it's easier to let the Devil steal a little of your soul, one bite at a time, and he is patient, but one day he will own you. It's always harder to be a good person and do the right thing even when it feels like you shouldn't; that's the Devil whispering in your ear.

I used to really feel the loss of friends or romantic partners because I loved them, and things felt magical. Then I realized I see the best in everybody.

They weren't the magic.

I WAS!

# Acknowledgement

I Was The Magic Sticker - Black Girl, Lost Keys. https://blackgirllostkeys.com/product/i-was-the-magic-sticker/

Fastelavn – the Nordic tradition you've probably never heard of. https://stptrans.com/fastelavn-the-nordic-tradition-youve-probably-never-heard-of/

Reborn as a Substitute Chapter 30 – YunYun Translations. https://yunyuntranslations.com/2022/03/24/reborn-as-a-substitute-chapter-30/

Sermons | Lutheran Church of the Cross. https://www.lutheranvictoria.ca/podcasts/media/2023-02-26-lent-1

Delvaux, Denise. "The Politics of Humanitarian Organizations Neutrality and Solidarity: The Case of the ICRC and MSF during the 1994 Rwandan Genocide." 2005, https://core.ac.uk/download/335386071.pdf.

Sermons | Lutheran Church of the Cross. https://www.lutheranvictoria.ca/podcasts/media/2023-02-26-lent-1

Printed in Poland
by Amazon Fulfillment
Poland Sp. z o.o., Wrocław
13 January 2024

81fac689-7a4e-46a7-b0fe-a5855f66d3dfR01